Anti-Security

Mark Neocleous & George S. Rigakos

Anti-Security

Mark Neocleous & George S. Rigakos

© Red Quill Books Ltd. 2011
Ottawa

www.redquillbooks.com

ISBN 978-1-926958-14-9

Printed on acid-free paper. The paper used in this book incorporates post-consumer waste and has not been sourced from endangered old growth forests, forests of exceptional conservation value or the Amazon Basin. Red Quill Books subscribes to a one-book-at-a-time manufacturing process that substantially lessens supply chain waste, reduces greenhouse emissions, and conserves valuable natural resources.

"Anti-Security"

Run by an editorial collective, Red Quill Books is dedicated to the following three principles:

1. Consciousness Raising: We are committed to disseminating critical academic works to a mass readership in formats that are accessible and that raise awareness and promote political engagement.

2. Ecology: We aim to build a sustainable and Green publishing house. Our processes are digital with minimal supply-chain waste. We are an on-demand producer of books, which also ensures our books are never out of print.

3. Community: We will be offering academic prizes and graduate research grants to support the next generation of critical scholars. We seek to actively promote future critical scholarship.

[RQB is a radical publishing house. Part of the proceeds from the sale of this book will support student scholarships.]

Introduction

In October 2010 a small group of academics and graduate students from disciplines ranging from sociology, politics and criminology to political economy and geography convened for two days at Carleton University, Ottawa, to present papers on policing, security and the possibility of critique. Unlike other workshops the aim was not only to engage in communicating about our recent research but also to contemplate what it might mean to challenge the hegemony of security. Part of this challenge lay first and foremost in the mix of disciplinary backgrounds of the people involved: our deliberate attempt to overcome the intellectual poverty brought about by the specializations under which the bourgeois academy operates. The other part of the challenge was to try and think through a politics of what we had started calling '*anti*-security'.

The discussion that ensued was energizing. Time was set aside to consider what it might mean to be involved in a political project of anti-security, and the implications this might have for our understanding of police power, political economy and the contemporary state. There was a general sense that considerations of security had reached an analytic blockage. Despite mounting dissatisfaction with measures enacted in its name, more security institutes were being formed, more security experts were being produced, and more social problems were being redefined as security matters. It was clear that police measures through pacification were being legitimized under the rubric of security. Far from being some kind of historical turning point, 9/11 was better understood as a milestone in the constant expansion and escalation of force and subjugation in the name of security.

To try and think about security these days is to risk being taken over by its logic. Even the most critical of the critical studies of security tend to succumb to the idea that security is a fundamental human need, well understood as the formula of 'life, liberty, security'. The state must therefore tend to this need. As such, security institutes and experts have tended to become little more than the intellectual wing of the security industry, serving to reinforce the security-oriented policies of the managerial state.

Security makes necessary all the things done in the name of security. If it is the case that as the ideas of the ruling class are in every epoch the ruling ideas – and if any notion can now lay claim to be the ruling idea it is surely 'security' – then the implications are clear: the huge body of work on security being produced within the Universities and think tanks is thus bourgeois ideology. As ever, the success of such ideology is best measured by the extent to which the ruling class manages to shape and order its opponents' thoughts and language; that is, by the extent to which even critical thinkers come to believe that they *shouldn't, mustn't,* and maybe even that they *can't* think in any other way. This constitutes perhaps the most significant hurdle for political engage-

Anti-Security
Edited by Mark Neocleous and
George Rigakos

ment on the Left, and part of the mood at the meeting was that a radical departure is needed from a discourse that continues to march unabated and unchallenged.

As the conveners we set about trying to condense and crystallize these discussions in the form of a brief statement, which took the form of a working document for circulation among the group and has morphed into the text which follows this Introduction: *Anti-Security: A Declaration*. The *Declaration* performed and performs a number of tasks. First, it initially reaffirmed our previous work and restates our desire to move critical - and particularly Marxist – assessments and challenges of security forward. Second, it served to act as a touchstone for the papers that have been included here, all of which take up from, develop, and, perhaps most importantly, supersede some of its aspects. Which is precisely how it was intended: as a starting point for critical reflection. And, third, the *Declaration* is intended as an invitation for further engagement in the project. It is meant as an opening, not a closing.

This opening is reflected in the fact that many of the papers in this collection have been radically transformed in the months after the meeting. In this sense, our collective engagement is intended to start something new: a call to other researchers, an invitation to analysts, activists, and critical thinkers to reassess their place within the security complex and to dare to think the impossible: to stand against security as it manifests itself under this mode of production, to consider what it might mean to be involved in *anti*-security.

Mark Neocleous and George Rigakos
June 2011

Contents

Introduction _ _ _ _ _ _ _ _ _ _ _ _ _ _ _ _ 7

Anti-Security: A Declaration _ _ _ _ _ _ _ _ _ 15

[1] Security as Pacification _ _ _ _ _ _ _ _ _ 23
Mark Neocleous

[2] 'To Extend the Scope of Productive Labour': Pacification as a Police Project _ _ 57
George S. Rigakos

[3] Public Policing, Private Security, Pacifying Populations _ _ _ _ _ _ _ _ _ 85
Michael Kempa

[4] War on the Poor: Urban Poverty, Target Policing and Social Control _ _ _ _ 107
Gaetan Heroux

[5] 'Poor Rogues' and Social Police: Subsistence Wages, Payday Lending and the Politics of Security _ _ _ _ _ _ _ 135
Olena Kobzar

[6] Liberal Intellectuals and the Politics of Security _ _ _ _ _ _ _ _ _ _ _ _ _ _ **165**
Will Jackson

[7] Security: Resistance _ _ _ _ _ _ _ _ _ _ **191**
Heidi Rimke

[8] Security and the Void: Aleatory Materialism contra Governmentality _ _ _ **217**
Ronjon Paul Datta

[9] 'All the People Necessary Will Die to Achieve Security' _ _ _ _ _ _ _ _ _ _ **243**
Guillermina Seri

Notes on contributors _ _ _ _ _ _ _ _ _ _ _ **267**

Anti-Security: A Declaration

THE PURPOSE OF THE PROJECT, PUT SIMPLY, IS TO SHOW THAT SECURITY IS AN ILLUSION THAT HAS FORGOTTEN IT IS AN ILLUSION. LESS SIMPLY, THAT SECURITY IS A *DANGEROUS* ILLUSION. WHY 'DANGEROUS'? BECAUSE IT HAS COME TO ACT AS A BLOCKAGE ON POLITICS: THE MORE WE SUCCUMB TO THE DISCOURSE OF SECURITY, THE LESS WE CAN SAY ABOUT EXPLOITATION AND ALIENATION; THE MORE WE TALK ABOUT SECURITY, THE LESS WE TALK ABOUT THE MATERIAL FOUNDATIONS OF EMANCIPATION; THE MORE WE COME TO SHARE IN THE FETISH OF SECURITY, THE MORE WE BECOME ALIENATED FROM ONE ANOTHER AND THE MORE WE BECOME COMPLICIT IN THE EXERCISE OF POLICE POWERS.

FLESHING OUT HOW WE GOT HERE IS THE FIRST CHALLENGE; SHOWING HOW DAMAGING THIS HAS BEEN IS AN EVEN GREATER CHALLENGE; DOING THESE THINGS IN A WAY THAT CONTRIBUTES TO A RADICAL, CRITICAL AND EMANCIPATORY POLITICS EVEN MORE SO. BUT IT IS A CHALLENGE THAT MUST BE MADE, AND MUST BE MADE COLLECTIVELY. AS A START, WE THEREFORE OFFER THE FOLLOWING DECLARATIONS ABOUT AN ANTI-SECURITY POLITICS.

WE DENY ALL FALSE BINARIES THAT OBFUSCATE AND REIFY THE SECURITY PROBLEMATIC AND SERVE ONLY TO REINFORCE ITS POWER. WE THEREFORE **REJECT**:

- LIBERTY VERSUS SECURITY: IN THE WORKS OF THE FOUNDERS OF THE LIBERAL TRADITION – THAT IS, THE FOUNDERS OF BOURGEOIS IDEOLOGY – LIBERTY IS SECURITY AND SECURITY IS LIBERTY. FOR THE RULING CLASS, SECURITY ALWAYS HAS AND ALWAYS WILL TRIUMPH OVER LIBERTY BECAUSE 'LIBERTY' HAS NEVER BEEN INTENDED AS A COUNTER-WEIGHT TO SECURITY. LIBERTY HAS ALWAYS BEEN SECURITY'S LAWYER.

- PUBLIC VERSUS PRIVATE: NO POST-HOC JURIDICAL DETERMINATION ABOUT ACCOUNTABILITY, LEGAL STANDING, UNIFORMING, OR LEGITIMATE USE OF FORCE CAN UNDO THE HISTORIC INTER-OPERABILITY OF PUBLIC AND PRIVATE POLICE, STATE AND MERCENARY ARMIES, CORPORATE AND GOVERNMENT SECURITY, OR TRANSNATIONAL CORPORATIONS AND INTERNATIONAL RELATIONS. THE PUBLIC SPHERE DOES THE WORK OF THE PRIVATE SPHERE, CIVIL SOCIETY THE WORK OF THE STATE. THE QUESTION IS THEREFORE NOT 'PUBLIC VERSUS PRIVATE' OR 'CIVIL

Anti-Security
Edited by Mark Neocleous and
George Rigakos

society versus the state', but the unity of bourgeois violence and the means by which pacification is legitimized in the name of security.

- SOFT VERSUS HARD: Such dichotomous constructions — soft versus hard policing for suppressing dissent; soft versus hard military intervention for stamping out local and indigenous resistance; soft versus hard power to impose global imperial hegemony — are but aspects of the unity of class violence, distracting us from universal pacification carried out in the name of capital.

- BARBARISM VERSUS CIVILIZATION: The history of civilization after the Enlightenment is the consolidation of wage labour, the cultural and material imposition of imperial domination, and the violence of class war. In the form of the 'standard of civilization' the majesty of the law was central to this project. To civilize is to project police power. 'Civilization' is code for enforcing capitalist relations; which is to say: bourgeois civilization is barbarism.

- DOMESTIC VERSUS FOREIGN: THE GREATEST TYRANNY OF SECURITY IS ITS INSISTENCE ON THE CONSTRUCTION OF THE 'OTHER'. SECURITY CREATES BOTH INTERNAL DOMESTIC AND EXTERNAL FOREIGN THREATS, GENERATING THE FEAR AND DIVISION THAT UNDERPINS RAISON D'ÉTAT. THE COLONIAL PACIFICATION OF SUBJECTS ABROAD IS SOON TURNED INTO DOMESTIC PACIFICATION OF SUBJECTS AT HOME. NEW *INTERNATIONAL* POLICING INITIATIVES ARE BUT A LABORATORY FOR THE MILITARIZATION OF *DOMESTIC* SECURITY. THE 'WAR ON TERROR' IS A PERMANENT MULTI-FRONT ASSAULT THAT LUMPS JIHADISTS WITH PEACENIKS, FEMINISTS WITH ISLAMISTS, AND SOCIALISTS WITH ASSASSINS. NO PRETENCE AT A DISTINCTION IS NECESSARY BECAUSE THE CAPITALIST STATE IS INSECURE IN ALL DIRECTIONS.

- PRE- AND POST-9/11: LET'S BE CLEAR: THE MURDER OF 3,000 ON SEPTEMBER 11, 2001 WAS HORRIFIC, BUT IT DID *NOT CHANGE ANYTHING*. TO BELIEVE SO IS TO ENGAGE IN A DELIBERATE ACT OF FORGETTING. THE SECURITY APPARATUS THAT REVVED UP IN THE DAYS AFTER THE ATTACK HAD BEEN IN THE MAKING FOR DECADES AS THE

TERRAIN OF THE CLASS WAR SHIFTED. THE TARGETS OF THE NEW 'WAR' – THIS TIME ON TERROR – WERE NOT NEW. THE CRY OF 'INSECURITY' WAS AGAIN ANSWERED WITH TWO FAMILIAR DEMANDS: YOU CONSUME, AND WE WILL DESTROY. GO TO DISNEYLAND, AND LET THE STATE CONTINUE THE WORK IT HAD BEEN CONDUCTING FOR GENERATIONS. IF 9/11 ACCOMPLISHED ANYTHING, IT WAS TO MAKE SECURITY ALL BUT UNASSAILABLE.

EXCEPTION AND NORMALITY: THIS IS *NOT* A STATE OF EXCEPTION. THE CAPITALIST STATE RIDING ROUGHSHOD OVER HUMAN RIGHTS IN THE NAME OF SECURITY IS NORMAL. THE RULING CLASS CARRYING OUT ACTS OF VIOLENCE IN THE NAME OF ACCUMULATION IS NORMAL. THE DEVISING OF NEW TECHNIQUES TO DISCIPLINE AND PUNISH RECALCITRANT SUBJECTS IS NORMAL. TARGETED ASSASSINATIONS, THE BOMBING OF CIVILIANS, IMPRISONMENT WITHOUT TRIAL.. NORMAL, NORMAL, NORMAL. AND, LEST WE FORGET: LIBERALS FALLING OVER THEMSELVES JUSTIFY SUCH THINGS? NORMAL.

Anti-Security: A Declaration

WE **UNDERSTAND** INSTEAD THAT SECURITY TODAY:

- OPERATES AS THE SUPREME CONCEPT OF BOURGEOIS SOCIETY.

- COLONIZES AND DE-RADICALIZES DISCOURSE: HUNGER TO FOOD SECURITY; IMPERIALISM TO ENERGY SECURITY; GLOBALIZATION TO SUPPLY CHAIN SECURITY; WELFARE TO SOCIAL SECURITY; PERSONAL SAFETY TO PRIVATE SECURITY. SECURITY MAKES BOURGEOIS ALL THAT IS INHERENTLY COMMUNAL. IT ALIENATES US FROM SOLUTIONS THAT ARE NATURALLY SOCIAL AND FORCES US TO SPEAK THE LANGUAGE OF STATE RATIONALITY, CORPORATE INTEREST, AND INDIVIDUAL EGOISM. INSTEAD OF SHARING, WE HOARD. INSTEAD OF HELPING, WE BUILD DEPENDENCIES. INSTEAD OF FEEDING OTHERS, WE LET THEM STARVE.. ALL IN THE NAME OF SECURITY.

- IS A SPECIAL COMMODITY, PLAYING A PIVOTAL ROLE IN THE EXPLOITATION, ALIENATION AND IMMISERATION OF WORKERS. IT PRODUCES ITS OWN *FETISH*, EMBEDDING ITSELF INTO ALL OTHER COMMODITIES, PRODUCING EVEN MORE RISK AND FEAR WHILE INTENSIFYING AND DISTRACTING US FROM THE MATERIAL CONDITIONS OF EXPLOITATION THAT HAVE

Anti-Security
Edited by Mark Neocleous and
George Rigakos

MADE US INHERENTLY INSECURE. IT MAKES CONCRETE OUR EPHEMERAL INSECURITIES UNDER CAPITALIST RELATIONS. IT ATTEMPTS TO SATIATE THROUGH CONSUMPTION WHAT CAN ONLY BE ACHIEVED THROUGH REVOLUTION.

THE **CALL** OF THIS *DECLARATION* IS THAT WE:

- NAME SECURITY FOR WHAT IT REALLY IS;

- STAND AGAINST THE SECURITIZATION OF POLITICAL DISCOURSE;

- CHALLENGE THE AUTHORITARIAN AND REACTIONARY NATURE OF SECURITY;

- POINT TO THE WAYS IN WHICH SECURITY POLITICS SHIFTS ATTENTION AWAY FROM MATERIAL CONDITIONS AND QUESTIONS, IN THE PROCESS TRANSFORMING EMANCIPATORY POLITICS INTO AN ARM OF POLICE;

- FIGHT FOR AN ALTERNATIVE POLITICAL LANGUAGE THAT TAKES US BEYOND THE NARROW HORIZON OF BOURGEOIS SECURITY AND ITS POLICE POWERS..

MARK NEOCLEOUS AND GEORGE RIGAKOS
NOVEMBER 2010

[1]
Security as Pacification

MARK_NEOCLEOUS

Early in *The Manifesto of the Communist Party*, Marx and Engels make the following claim:

> The bourgeoisie cannot exist without constantly revolutionising the instruments of production, and thereby the relations of production, and with them the whole relations of society. Conservation of the old modes of production in unaltered form, was, on the contrary, the first condition of existence for all earlier industrial classes. Constant revolutionising of production, uninterrupted disturbance of all social conditions, everlasting uncertainty and agitation distinguish the bourgeois epoch from all earlier ones. All fixed, fast-frozen relations, with their train of ancient and venerable prejudices and opinions, are swept away, all new-formed ones become antiquated before they can ossify. All that is solid melts into air.

Understood in terms of what has become the most important political trope of contemporary politics, the suggestion seems to be that at some fundamental level the order of capital is an order of social *insecurity*. Yet this permanent insecurity gives rise to a *politics of security*, turning security into the fundamental concept of bourgeois society. It is through this politics of security that the constant revolutionising of production and uninterrupted disturbance of capitalist order is fabricated, structured and administered. This, I suggest, is the process of pacification.

Anti-Security
Edited by Mark Neocleous and
George Rigakos

Little is said about pacification at all these days. This is perhaps because of the association of the term with the American-Vietnam war: following its adoption by the US state in 1964-5 as a substitute term for 'counter-insurgency', 'pacification' became key to US strategy in Vietnam, and thereby gave the term very strong imperial-military connotations making it appear best suited to the world of IR and strategic studies. Yet even military terminology has now shifted away from 'pacification' towards more subtle terms such as 'low-intensity conflict', 'operations other than war', and the 'gray area phenomenon' - the recently revised US Army and Marine Corps *Counterinsurgency Field Manual* (2006), for example, makes passing reference to pacification then subsumes this under the broader targets which counterinsurgency is meant to achieve: police and security.

So why try to think security through a category which once scored so highly on the military register but which even the military register has now replaced? Because 'fundamental to pacification is security'. This comment from General William C. Westmoreland, reflecting on his experience of the pacification efforts during Vietnam, is a far from unusual comment for the period. Robert McNamara, US Secretary of Defense during the same war, described the war as a 'pacification security job', and Robert W. Komer, Special Assistant for Pacification from 1966 to 1968, suggested that 'security is the key to pacification'.[1] It has been easy for scholars to pass over such comments as specific to the conflict in Vietnam or as just one more assertion of the abstract idea that war is conducted in the name of security. In fact, I think there is more at stake. Because if, as has been argued elsewhere, we need to understand security not as some kind of universal or transcendental value but rather as a mode of governing or a political technology of liberal order-building, then perhaps the category of pacification can help us make more sense of this process. To see security as a constitutive power or a technique deployed and mobilized in the exercise of power is to read it as a *police* mechanism: a mechanism for the fabrication of a social order organized around a constant revolutionising of the instruments and relations of production and thus containing the everlasting uncertainty and agitation of all social relations that Marx and Engels define as key to capitalism. I therefore want to tease out of the language of pacification an argument concerning the power of the state in securing the insecurity of capitalist accumulation. In so doing I want to make a wider theoretical suggestion: that for tactical purposes critical theory really needs to re-appropriate the term 'pacification' to help grasp the nature of security politics.

Pacification: model

In 1970 a report was published by the RAND organization called *Organization and Management of the "New Model" Pacification Program*. Written by Komer and detailing the developments in Vietnam from 1966 (when the 'new model' program replaced the 'old model' of counter-insurgency), the Report highlights the relationship between pacification and security, but notes that this concerns much more than territorial

Anti-Security
Edited by Mark Neocleous and
George Rigakos

security. Rather, the relationship incorporates 'a series of interlocking programs' concerning land reform, economic development, roads and communications. The idea of the 'restoration' of security was important, then - 'pacification required first and foremost the restoration of security', noted Komer - but the restoration was to be a civil-military joint action affecting the everyday life of the Vietnamese. The military struggle against insurgency was only one dimension of a much larger project to 'create a socio-political environment in which future insurgency would not flourish again'; an environment in which Vietnamese life would have to be restructured in order to prevent communism. In other words, pacification touches on the fundamental nature of security in its most expansive sense, involving 'police-type actions and constructive politico-economic programs as security is restored'.[2]

I will return to the American pacification of Vietnam in a moment. But let us note here that the US went in to Vietnam on the back of French failure in the same region and that France had been there for a century as part of its contribution to the European colonizing spree of the nineteenth century. During this time the French did more than their fair share of thinking about what makes for successful colonization. In this regard an article called 'Du role colonial de l'Armée' by Lieutenant Colonel Lyautey and first published in 1900 played an important role; so important, in fact, that when half a century later the French were failing in Vietnam and the Americans were gearing up to step in, French colonial thinking was still dominated by the article. Much of the article consists of quotes from the set of instructions on colonial rule issued in 1898 by

General Galliéni, the governor of Madagascar and a leading strategist of French colonial warfare, and the instructions themselves were published by Galliéni in *Rapport d'ensemble sur la pacification, l'organisation et la colonisation de Madagascar*. Note the connection in the title between pacification and colonization.

'The best means for achieving pacification in our new colony is provided by combined application of force and politics', notes Galliéni. By 'force' and 'politics' he means 'destruction' and 'reconstruction' respectively.

> It must be remembered that, in the course of colonial struggles, we should turn to destruction only as a last resort and only as a preliminary to better reconstruction. We must always treat the country and its inhabitants with consideration, since the former is destined to receive our future colonial enterprises and the latter will be our main agents and collaborators in the development of our enterprises. Every time that the necessities of war force one of our colonial officers to take action against a village or an inhabited center, his first concern, once submission of the inhabitants has been achieved, should be reconstruction of the village, creation of a market, and the establishment of a school.

Destruction and 'reconstruction' go hand-in-hand. Yet although 'it is by combined use of politics and force that pacification of a country and its future organization will be achieved', it is 'political action [that] is by

Anti-Security
Edited by Mark Neocleous and
George Rigakos

far the more important', deriving as it does 'from the organization of the country and its inhabitants'. Thus it is the politics/reconstruction that counts, because this is where real pacification lies.

> As pacification gains ground, the country becomes more civilized, markets are reopened, trade is reestablished. The role of the soldier becomes of secondary importance. The activity of the administrator begins. It is necessary, on the one hand, to study and satisfy the social requirements of the subject people and, on the other hand, to promote the development of colonization, which will utilize the natural resources of the soil and open the outlets for European trade.
>
> Moreover, circumstances inevitably impose these obligations. A country is not conquered and pacified when a military operation has decimated and terrorized its people. Once the initial shock passes, a spirit of revolt will arise among the masses, fanned by a feeling of resentment which has been created by the application of brute force.

Note: as 'the role of the soldier becomes of secondary importance' so 'the activity of the administrator begins'. Or as Lyautey puts it in his gloss on this argument: 'during the period following the conquest, the part of the troops is reduced to policing, a function which is soon taken over by special troops, the military and civilian police'.[3]

By the mid-twentieth century Gallieni and Lyautey's suggestions from the turn of the century were being revived: 'Between the Lyauteyan pacifications and the French colonial experience of the 1950s there is an undisguised doctrinal continuum'.[4] This was most notable in the idea that soldiers should perform civic duties, which led to the creation of the Specialized Administrative Sections (SAS) in Algeria, tasked with supervising work, food distribution, medical aid, reconstruction and resettlement, and the establishment of a Centre for Instruction and Preparation in Counterinsurgency-Guerrilla Warfare (CIPCG), through which approximately 10,000 officers were educated in ideological warfare, psychological manipulation and police action. The lessons learnt were the same as those learnt by the British in their pacification of Malaysia, Cyprus and Kenya.

Thus by the time the Americans were ready to rethink their war in Vietnam as a war of *pacification*, they had to hand a long history of thinking about this process as a principle of social reconstruction and as the conjunction of military and police functions. In this light, in 1960 the journal *Military Review*, at that point the major theoretical journal of the US army, ran an article suggesting that 'the French experience and its contingent problems are worth the most carefully detailed scrutiny by our qualified military experts',[5] and followed this with a series of articles through the early-1960s. The Americans had also translated Roger Trinquier's *La Guerre Moderne*, a series of reflections of Trinquier's experience of French pacification work - the term 'modern warfare' in his title was in fact code for 'revolutionary warfare' - and first published in France in 1961. For Trinquier, 'warfare is now an interlocking system of actions – political, economic, psychological, military'.[6] Similarly, in 1963 the RAND Corporation commissioned David Galula to write about the French pacification of Algeria. Galula had been a Captain and then Lieutenant Colonel in the French Army and overseen a large part of the pacification of Algeria, having previously experienced similar wars in China, the Philippines, Malaysia and Greece, and his work had an important impact on American thinking about the pacification of Vietnam (and, as we shall see, continues to shape thinking in the 'war on terror'). In his report on the pacification of Algeria he had made much of an approach based on 'the carrot in our left hand ... the stick in our right hand'.[7] The opportunity created by RAND allowed him to expand on this.

> The general directives from Robert Lacoste, the Minister-Resident in Algiers ... insisted on the need to win over the population. In my zone, as everywhere in Algeria, the order was to 'pacify'. But exactly how? The sad truth was that, in spite of all our past experience, we had no single, official doctrine for counterinsurgency warfare. Instead, there were various schools of thought, all unofficial, some highly vociferous ... At one extreme stood the 'warriors', officers who had learned nothing, who challenged the very idea that the population was the real objective, who maintained that military action pursued with sufficient vigor and for a sufficiently long time would defeat the rebels ...

At the other extreme were the 'psychologists', most of them recruited among officers who had undergone the Vietminh brainwashing in prisoner camps. To them, psychological action was everything, not merely the simple propaganda and psychological warfare adjunct to other types of operations, conventional or otherwise. 'You use force against the enemy', one of their leaders told me, 'not so much to destroy him but in order to make him change his mind on the necessity of pursuing the fight. In other words, you do a psychological action'. They were convinced that the population could be manipulated through certain techniques adapted from communist methods.[8]

The report thus spends the majority of its time talking about the struggle to gain the control and support of the population through 'pacification units' based in 'pacification zones' and using medical, educational and ideological efforts, all in the name of 'security'. A year later, Galula developed his arguments into a book called *Counterinsurgency Warfare: Theory and Practice*.[9]

My main concern, however, is not how much the experience of other colonial powers was known to the Americans, but in how we might think the relationship between pacification and security. For as much as the term 'pacification' to describe American actions in Vietnam might in one sense be 'a dishonest misnomer ... [for] a policy characterised by repression, torture and murder',[10] the fact that it was thought of and understood in terms of a myth of reconstruction,

Anti-Security
Edited by Mark Neocleous and
George Rigakos

and a myth of reconstruction centred on 'security', is nonetheless still important, not least because this is the moment in which the national security apparatus was being ratcheted up.

'Pacification had to be productive', notes William Gibson in his history of the US 'Technowar' war in Vietnam.[11] 'Productive' in the sense that it had to imply the construction of a new social order as well as the crushing of opposition to that construction. To this end, soldiers became 'pacification workers' organized as Combined Action Platoons (CAPs) as part of the strategy known as Civil Operations and Revolutionary Development Support (CORDS). Working on a broad principle of security and led largely by personnel from the American security elite, such as William Colby of the CIA, CORDS went about trying to reorganize the whole of Vietnamese society. This included efforts to protect and develop rural areas, revive the economy, and provide health and educational services. Much of this involved fundamentally bourgeois assumptions about what might count as 'peace and security' - the country was saturated with ideological slogans and advertisements for commodities, cultural and ideological production was transformed in the attempt to win 'hearts and minds', the economy was to be 'modernized' and even sexuality was to be mobilized through the use of 'erotic' pamphlets showing the beauty of western liberty. But the real point is that this was a huge effort to express the 'productive' dimension of what President Johnson called 'the other war': 'a war to build as well as to destroy'. 'Nation building', as the 1970 RAND report put it.[12]

This explains the various names under which pacification was conducted: Reconstruction, Rural Construction, Revolutionary Reconstruction, Land Development, Civic Action, and so on. Some of these were even run together with 'pacification', on the lines of 'Rural Construction/Pacification' or 'pacification/rural development'. One contemporary comments that 'in the term's most common meaning – physical security – most of South Vietnam is pacified', but then discusses pacification as including 'general living conditions' such as housing, food and clothing, schooling, health, village life, and compares the everyday life of the Vietnamese under the Viet Cong and American rule.[13] Thus the project of reconstruction is understood as the project of security which is in turn understood as pacification. One Report called *Pacification Measurement in Vietnam* offers a 'Hamlet Evaluation Worksheet', with 18 indicators grouped under six basic factors, generating a final 'hamlet security score' according to the level of 'development'. Hence development and security are essentially rolled together to the point where hamlets are finally measured according to their 'security or development hamlet scores' and their 'security and developmental status'. The Report's conclusions are thus that the Hamlet Evaluation System is a 'reliable technique for measuring the key aspects of pacification that are measurable - hamlet population, security and development'.[14]

This is a theme that runs through the secondary literature of the period too. Geoffrey Fairbairn, to give just one example, comments on pacification in terms of the 'problem of security', but adds that this problem was to be dealt with through a panoply of measures 'producing radical and constructive change in the lives of the people'.[15] Hence in summing up the 'Eleven Criteria and Ninety-Eight Works for Pacification' in Vietnam, Gibson notes that 'the list sounds like a program for the construction of a liberal welfare state'. A liberal welfare state indeed, but one in which the violence of the state power underpinning its construction was far more apparent. So apparent, in fact, that it should be understood as a 'militarized market regime' intent on producing a 'modern' distribution of persons and commodities.[16]

The 'pacification security job' in Vietnam can thus certainly be understood as military violence to crush a people and secure a nation; the terror bombing resulting in an estimated 1.5 to 2.5 million dead Vietnamese and involving some 7 million tons of bombs and artillery grenades dropped by 1975 are ample testimony to that. But it also has to be understood in terms of the *liberal security measures* through which the people were to be 'reconstructed' and the nation 'rebuilt'. As with many practices carried out under the banner of 'security', the pacification program in Vietnam embodied a fairly standard mixture of tough-minded force and a far more amorphous liberal rhetoric of construction and reconstruction: 'touchy-feely domination', as Jacobsen calls it.[17] This domination through 'hearts and minds' and the reconstruction of the nation around bourgeois notions of order is a key dimension of most forms of imperialism.[18] It is pacification as a political technology for organizing everyday life through the production and re-organization of the ideal citizen-subjects of capitalism. Or as one minister of Revolutionary Development in Vietnam put it, pacification aims not only at destroying 'the present, gloomy *old life*', but also 'replacing it with a *brighter and nicer new life*',[19] the kind of brighter and nicer life identified by Marx and Engels as the animating feature of the bourgeois world: the constant disturbance of all social conditions, the unremitting uncertainty and agitation of all human ties, the melting away of all that is solid into air. As they also note in the same section of the *Manifesto*, so powerful is the bourgeois need for this form of social order that it chases the dream over the whole surface of the earth, creating a world after its own image. The pacification of Vietnam is but one instance of this creation.

Pacification: history

Because of its predominance during the US actions in Vietnam, 'pacification' is a term closely associated with that war. In fact, the first real extended treatment of pacification comes in Captain Bernardo de Vargas Machuca's *Milicia Indiana*, published in 1599. It is notable that this text, which is to all intents and purposes the world's first manual of counter-revolutionary warfare, appears amidst the so-called 'military revolution of the sixteenth century', since Machuca's arguments identify pacification as a feature of war that has been omitted from the standard accounts of the military revolution, which focus on the centralization of violence and the bureaucratization and discipline of standing armies. The Spaniards, like all major powers of the sixteenth century, were indeed immersed in a world of large scale military engagement; yet, also like the other major powers, they were simultaneously immersed in the colonization of other lands. This colonization required a very different kind of political violence. It is in this light that Machuca writes his manual of Indian military encounters. As one of the few writers to note the significance of the manual notes, 'Machuca dismissed as irrelevant the entire pattern of European warfare, with its hierarchical tactical units, linear formations, and permanent garrisons. Instead he advocated for the Americas the creation of commando groups to carry out search-and-destroy missions deep within enemy territory for up to two years at a time'. Success required knowledge and experience as much in 'planting survival crops and curing tropical ulcers as about laying ambushes and mounting surprise attacks'. Through 'the adoption of native methods, the colonial frontier ... was steadily consolidated, and warfare there became "nothing but a manhunt" (in the phrase of a Jesuit contemporary), in which the settlers hunted down recalcitrant Indians with mastiffs and knives'.[20] Machuca's concern was not that of one militarily organised national unit facing another, but of an Empire confronting recalcitrant and rebellious indigenous populations. To fight these populations Machuca advocated adopting their fighting methods, learned by him 'after twenty-eight years ... employed in pacifications in the Indies'. The manual thus describes a world of skirmishing and ambushing, of fighting on the move, of a 24-hour 'hunt' against enemy 'hunters'. This is the war of militias as part of an expanding global empire. It is a war for the pacification of those peoples which empire would necessarily have to destroy or control.[21]

The pacification in question is thus on the one hand brutal and bloody, with what we now know to be fairly standard atrocities associated with colonialism, including the burning alive of rebels, summary executions and the occasional drowning of babies, all justified by Machuca in the familiar terms of colonial conquest: because the war is just, because the Indian rebellion requires punishment, and because the Indians are 'with no reason, depraved and without honor' and are 'even more brutish than irrational animals'. On the other hand, Machuca insists that 'fair treatment' must be granted the Indian: the 'distributing and assigning the Indians to their encomiendas' must be done with the approval of the native lords of the land, the Indians should be granted herds, gifts, and care, commanders must carry out censuses. Most of all, they must be governed in 'peace'.[22]

Why did such a text emerge at this historical moment? The *Oxford English Dictionary* cites the Edicts of Pacification of 1563, 1570 and the Edict of Nantes in 1598 as the first examples of the word 'pacification', where it describes the powers used by a prince or state 'to put an end to strife or discontent' and 'to reduce to peaceful submission' a population. The dates are important, since they are deep into the period of early global accumulation and the history of capital; in other words, they are the point of departure for the period in which the insecurity of bourgeois order had to be secured. In this context, Philip II came to believe that the violence being meted out in the conquest of the colonies was causing a certain discontent among his own people. He therefore proclaimed in July 1573 that all further extensions of empire be termed 'pacifications' rather than 'conquests'.

> Discoveries are not to be called conquests. Since we wish them to be carried out peacefully and charitably, we do not want the use of the term 'conquest' to offer any excuse for the employment of force or the causing of injury to the Indians ... Without displaying any greed for the possessions of the Indians, they [the 'discoverers', 'conquerors'] are to establish friendship and cooperation with the lords and nobles who seem most likely to be of assistance in the pacification of the land.[23]

The history of 'discovery' as an ideological gloss on conquest and dispossession is too well known to bear repeating here. But Philip's use of the term 'pacification' is historically significant. Witness the ordinances issued in this regard, since they set in train the kind of practices that would still be running over 400 years later:

> They [the pacifiers/conquerors] are to gather information about the various tribes, languages and divisions of the Indians in the province ... They are to seek friendship with them through trade and barter, showing them great love and tenderness and giving them objects to which they will take a liking ... In order that the Indians may hear the faith with greater awe

and reverence, the preachers should convey the Cross in their hands and should be wearing at least albs or stoles ... The preachers should ask for their children under the pretext of teaching them and keep them as hostages; they should also persuade them to build churches where they can teach so that they may be safer. By these and other means are the Indians to be pacified and indoctrinated, but in no way are they to be harmed, for all we seek is their welfare and their conversion.[24]

Is this a military act? Clearly yes, in the sense that the armed force behind it is obvious. Yet it also concerns the gathering of information about the population, the teaching of trades, education, welfare provision, ideological indoctrination, and, most importantly, the construction of a market. These activities concern the practices of everyday life constitutive of human subjectivity and social order. They are the practices we associate with the police power: the dispersal of the mythical entity called 'security' through civil society and the fabrication of order around the logic of peace and security. This is pacification through the police of the everyday insecurities of life organised around accumulation and money and which would, from this point on, remain central to the colonial enterprise.

And not just the colonial enterprise: for it is pertinent that at this very moment historically the structural transformation of the state and original accumulation were having a 'domestic' impact. The growth of towns generated concern over forms of behaviour made possible by urbanization: gambling, drinking, adultery, blasphemy and, of course, the 'wandering' poor causing disorder and insecurity. Fears were increasingly expressed about a 'dissolute condition of masterlesse men', as Hobbes puts it, created from the collapse of feudal order, 'without subjection to Lawes', and thus wandering in a disorderly fashion with no 'coercive Power to tye their hands'. Worse, such creatures were thought to be behind the rise of popular disturbances throughout Europe. In the terms of the new political discourse emerging around the state and the new regime of accumulation, this conjunction of 'disorderliness' and 'criminality' was connected to the idea of 'rebellion' against the very structures of life and modes of being that were being imposed and even against the political order itself. Together, the 'criminal-disorderly-rebel' constituted the *lawless* creature - according to the *Oxford English Dictionary* this is the period that 'lawlessness' becomes widely used, pertaining to 'disorderly' and 'disobedience' as well as the absence of law. And this lawless creature constituted *the* security problem of the age. It is at this moment that the process of *internal pacification* begins, a process fabricating a 'peace and security' within the social order (i.e. 'homeland security') to match the 'peace and security' imposed on colonial subjects. The increased concentration of military power that comes with the bureaucratic military structure and professional standing armies was necessary not only for warfare against distant enemies similarly organised, but also for the permanent pacification of the internal territory.[25] Which is to say: it has to be understood *in terms of the logic of security* as a whole: the construction of elaborate security structures targeting civilian populations in general and 'suspect communities' or the 'enemy within' in particular.

Now, this process was worked out in different ways in different states, but the general tendency is clear: the process as a whole facilitated a functional integration of the pacifying powers of the modern state, with the military and police powers unified around the logic of pacification. This logic of internal pacification is not just about the violent crushing of opposition (though it certainly involves that), nor just a question of which 'force' does the crushing (military, paramilitary, police?), but is also very much about the shaping of the behaviour of individuals, groups, and classes, and thereby ordering the social relations of power around a particular regime of accumulation. In other words, what is at stake in pacification is the kind of security measure that lies at the heart of the fabrication of social order. The growth of bureaucracy and the rise of pacification went hand-in-hand as 'order' and 'security' became the key terms around which the bureaucracy was organised and the pacification carried out. The idea of security was central to the creation of what Elias calls the 'durably pacified social spaces'.[26] Conversely, the creation of durably pacified social spaces was central to the politics of security. The security of pacified social space is perhaps the key feature of bourgeois modernity. At the same time, violence is gradually eradicated from the dominant economic relations as feudal forms of power and authority are gradually replaced by the economic compulsion of the far more 'peaceful' bourgeois labour contract (masking, of course, the real violence of class war).

What we have, then, is a thread connecting the US project in Vietnam to nineteenth century European colonialism and beyond, all the way back to the European colonization of America in the sixteenth century: the thread of pacification. And this thread grasps pacification as a security job, understands that this security job reverberates through the everyday lives of the pacified, and sees this as oscillating from the colonies to the domestic scene and back again. The thread, in other words, reminds us that pacification concerns the police power and its central role in the fabrication of social order, that the core logic of police power is peace and security, and that the war machine that is the state and capital is to be organised around this logic. It reminds us that the insecurity of bourgeois order must be permanently secured.

Pacification: present

I realise that it is a thread that many will find too speculative. So let me push the speculation even further and bring the argument forward to the 'war on terror'. But let me do so via a consideration of the gamut of 'wars' declared against enemies within, such as the wars on drugs, crime and poverty. Too many people, but most notably criminologists, have too often approached this gamut of wars by treating them as metaphorical, relying on a very conventional conception of what 'counts' as a war, namely, militarily organized states fighting each other.[27] In fact, we might be better off thinking of such wars as 'pacification security jobs'.

It has long been the case that warfare abroad is linked, politically, ideologically, technologically, and industrially, to the maintenance of order at home; conversely, that order abroad often means warfare at home. This is not, however, some by-product of war but is, rather, a deliberate ploy to ensure that the state can keep its own citizen-subjects pacified. This is the point at which 'war' and 'class war' meet. The war on drugs, for example, has always been series of related conflicts, some of which might centre on the production and use of drugs and the dictators who oversee the centres of production, but most of which involve crushing political opposition movements, disciplining subjects and justifying to the public new forms of warfare and the new technologies by which this warfare is to be conducted. In Columbia the war on drugs (and now the war on terror) has long provided a pretext for a permanent counter-insurgency strategy. The war on drugs there has been used to justify the continued funding of the Columbian military by the US 'so that it can pacify those armed groups and unarmed progressive social forces that potentially threaten a stability geared towards US interests'.[28] Thus in Columbia as elsewhere, the war on drugs has at various moments slipped into and out of the war on communism, the war on terror and the war on crime in general (though these are never entirely distinguishable). In essence, however, the main purpose of this permanent and permanently shifting war has been to 'secure those parts of the country which are rich in natural resources for Colombian landowners and foreign multinationals'. The main function of the Columbian army has been making the country safe for capital accumulation. 'That is why, over the past ten years, the paramilitaries it works with have killed some 15,000 trades unionists, peasant and indigenous leaders, human rights workers, land reform activists, leftwing politicians and their sympathisers'.[29] With this broader remit the drugs war is always already incorporated into the global system of war, carried out through direct military engagement with nations, 'drug lords' and drug smuggling gangs but also employing an array of measures once part and parcel of colonial warfare.[30]

Seen in this light it is unsurprising that the dominant strategic theme of the war on drugs has been security. Nixon, Reagan and Bush all thought and fought the war on the grounds of security, and more recent politicians have followed suit. Drugs were formally defined as a national security problem (for example, in the 1986 National Security Decision Directive signed by Reagan) and the 'security services' have been centrally involved in the war. At the same time, we need to note that the security logic underpinning the war on drugs means that the war slips from the inside to the outside and back again, folding the foreign and domestic, the international and the everyday, into one another. The drugs war is a means by which the 'low-intensity conflict' of pacification is brought back into the domestic frame, via a replication of one of the fundamental tropes of security discourse: the articulation of an 'emergency situation' with a 'clear and present danger' threatening the fundamental fabric of society.[31] Playing heavily on the 'law and order' agenda, the war on drugs provides a rationale for coercive powers exercised within and across the face of civil society, for extensive penal control of categories of population regarded as dangerous, and for the growth of exclusion zones, social fortressing and the militarization of urban spaces. With the declaration of martial law in drug-producing countries replicated by the increasing use of emergency powers within liberal democracies, the war has paved the way for the pacification of groups perceived as the least useful and most dangerous parts of the population, of regions regarded as 'ungovernable' and borders regarded as 'insecure'. The outcome has been nothing less than guerrilla campaigns of penal harassment directly targeted on dispossessed neighbourhoods in the decaying urban core.[32]

This targeting was heavily mediated by sets of assumptions about race and class. The race issues endemic to the military and diplomatic battle with non-Western states and political formations filtersinto every stage of the pacification process - legislation, arrest, conviction and sentencing. Writing about the drugs war in the US interior, Michael Tonry notes that the Generals in the war knew from the outset that drug use was falling among the vast majority of the population, but not among disadvantaged members of the urban underclass. As drugs increasingly came to be seen as dangerous and deviant, the danger and deviance came to be associated with sections of the working class and the racial 'underclass': 'in the 1920s, it was blacks and cocaine. In the 1930s, images of Mexicans and marijuana were prominent ... In the anti-drug hysteria of the 1980s, crack cocaine, the emblematic drug of the latest "war", is associated in public imagery with disadvantaged minority residents of the inner cities'. Thus 'anyone who knew the history of American drug policy could have foreseen that this war on drugs would target and mostly engage young disadvantaged members of minority groups as the enemy'.[33] Unsurprisingly, as in any war, countless lives were destroyed as the whole range of state power was used to arrest, prosecute, convict, and imprison the offending enemy. The range of measures taken means that the war on drugs can only be understood if one understands it as a form of low-intensity urban warfare carried out by the state in the name of security.

Such low-intensity warfare is also apparent in the wider war on crime, the real impact of which is felt hardest by those at the wrong end of the new police measures in the city and which also appears to be identical to the war on drugs: to increase the prison population, especially of working class and black people. Even the war on poverty can be read as a pacification measure activated through the power of 'social security': 'a war waged with many weapons', notes one of the war's historians, weapons 'such as withholding the opportunities for decent jobs, schools, housing'. But, he adds, 'sometimes it is also a killing war'.[34] Hence the conclusion of the 1996 *Report of the National Criminal Justice Commission*, after two years research and two hundred pages of analysis, that the criminal justice system seems to be 'front line' in the war on drugs and crimes, and that 'the enemy in this war is *our own people*'.[35]

These are wars in which the battleground is the security of everyday life; wars in which the 'gloomy old' everyday practices of some lives must be destroyed and replaced with 'brighter and nicer new lives'; wars against suspect communities defined as such by the state itself and said to be making the territory insecure; wars in the form of acts of security in which the state reasserts its being *as a state* by insisting on itself as *the* political mechanism for the fabrication of social order; wars as 'pacification security jobs'.

What then of the 'war on terror'? As is well known, many have suggested that this is an absurd war, since: a) one can't conduct war against a noun; and b) one might never know when the war is won. But this misses the point, which is that the 'war on terror' is a war of pacification and thus not a war in the terms of the 'grand wars' of the twentieth century. As the latest and most universal version of the formula 'war on …x', the 'war on terror' is part and parcel of the hypertrophied concepts of war and security that is part of the texture of Western modernity.[36] The continual oscillation over the extent to which the 'war on terror' is a war conducted against an enemy which also exists as a 'suspect community' within, an enemy which figures as military threat but which commits criminal acts, an enemy which is a war criminal but also a criminal at war, opens the door for the state to ratchet up police powers and remodel expectations about political rights, individual liberties and social freedoms, all in the name of security. The fact that one might never know when the war is won is thus not some kind of intellectual or political error on the part of the states conducting the war but is in fact a *deliberate political strategy*, since it acts as a mode of political administration for managing 'problem' subjects so as to include not just the occupation of cities and nations across the earth, but also the incarceration of people without trial, the practice of torture, and the eradication of fundamental liberties and hopes of resistance at home. Because the suspect communities are always already among us, we are all under suspicion, all potentially guilty, in ways which impact on our everyday lives: the requirement that we continually engage in patriotic acts; the 'information awareness' projects involving our bank accounts, insurance policies, travel arrangements and car rental agreements; the CCTV cameras monitoring our movements across towns and cities; the new rules for workplaces requiring us to act as 'immigration' (viz., 'security') officers as much as workers; the expectation that our use of libraries and the internet might be under permanent surveillance; the generalized cultural acceptance of security guards here there and everywhere; the moulding of social intercourse so that friends, families and lovers might report each other for any 'unusual' behaviour; the list goes on and on. These are the changes connecting everyday insecurities with the nomos of the earth; changes enabling the production of political docility in the name of security; changes revealing the 'war on terror' to be a war of pacification securing capital accumulation and thus the insecurity of bourgeois order; changes, that is, for the permanent pacification … of us.

Coda

If this argument has any weight then it suggests that 'pacification' should be a crucial term in helping us grasp what takes place as 'war', what passes as the current configuration of state power, and what is imposed as the political management of (in)security. I am therefore suggesting that far from being an idea whose time has past with the closing of the American war in/on Vietnam, the category 'pacification' in fact carries a powerful theoretical charge, linking as it does the military to the police, the foreign to the domestic, the colonial to the homeland. In other words, I am proposing as a tactical move that critical theory re-appropriates the concept of pacification to help grasp what takes place under the rubric of security politics. Perhaps this is the very reason why the US Army and Marine Corps *Counterinsurgency Field Manual* mentions pacification in passing but then quickly circumvents any discussion of it; maybe the US state knows that the concept 'pacification' really does reveal too much about modern power. On that note, let me close with two observations-cum-suggestions.

In her introduction to the University of Chicago Press edition of the *Manual*, Sarah Sewall, Director of the Carr Center for Human Rights Policy at Harvard University, notes that the *Manual* 'incorporates insights from French counterinsurgency guru David Galula'. We have already noted Galula's work as an intellectual link between the French pacification of Algeria and Indo-China and the American pacification of Vietnam, and noted that his work was published in two documents in 1963 and 1964. Here, we might add that Galula's long RAND article of 1963 was republished as a book in 2006 by Praeger in the US. In the same year the same publisher also reissued Galula's 1964 text *Counterinsurgency Warfare: Theory and Practice*, as well as a new edition of Trinquier's *Modern Warfare*.

My first closing observation is thus that the movers and shakers of the US state know full well that pacification is back on the agenda and are mining the historical sources for insights. I suggest that critical theory needs to do the same.

Done properly, such mining can unearth some real gems about security as pacification. Take the 'new' terminology in the field, such as Human Terrain System (HTS). HTS is much the rage these days in debates about the nature of military action, suggesting as it does that military work really need to engage on the 'human' as much as the 'physical' terrain and encouraging us to believe that it is 'human security' that is ultimately at stake. HTS has been described by Army historians and military personnel as 'a CORDS for the 21st century'.[37] It too is based loosely on Galula's work, and has its own history in imperial warfare. But as a category, 'human terrain' was first placed on the political agenda in terms of guerrilla warfare on the domestic front. In May 1968 the House Un-American Activities Committee published a report called *Guerrilla Warfare Advocates in the United States*. What did the HUAC suggest, in those heady days of revolutionary fervour? It suggested that the kind of guerrilla warfare advocated by Mao in China and Giap in Vietnam was also found at home: in the struggle of communists and black liberation movements (the concept of 'black terrorism' dates to the period from 1967 onwards).[38] It included an appendix by Geoffrey Fairbairn, who we encountered above writing about the pacification of Vietnam as a security measure, which suggested that guerrilla warfare is a form of warfare 'carried out by irregular forces' and in which the real struggle concerns 'control of the human terrain'.[39] Four years later Robert Moss of the International Institute for Strategic Studies published a book in which he criticized the guerrillas for 'their failure to study the human terrain'.[40] Much as his book was concerned with the guerrilla war against the US, his real concern was the need to pacify the radical elements of the American population. Hence the title: *The War for the Cities* – not Hanoi or Baghdad, but New York and Washington. In the British context, one might note that this is the period in which Frank Kitson's *Low Intensity Operations: Subversion, Insurgency, Peace-keeping* (1971), first published by commercial publishers but with the copyright under Her Majesty's Stationers Office, caused a storm by suggesting that British colonial counter-insurgency measures needed to be used for domestic pacification.[41]

My second observation-cum-suggestion, then, is that subsumed under the new language of military intervention is nothing less than the pacification of domestic as well as imperial resistance, the 'enemy within' as well as the 'enemy without', as security moves back and forth between the national and the international, as the urban crisis gets redefined as a national security crisis and vice versa. Critical theory needs the concept of pacification to make sense of this. And radicals need to understand that in the violent process through which bourgeois order is constituted, security *is* pacification.

Notes

1 General Westmoreland, *A Soldier Reports* (New York: Doubleday, 1976), p. 68; Robert McNamara, 'Memorandum to the President', 14 October, 1966, in *The Pentagon Papers, Gravel Edition, Vol. 2* (Boston: Beacon Press, 1971), p. 596; Robert Komer, 'Memorandum to the President' (no date), in *Pentagon Papers*, p. 570.

2 R. W. Komer, *Organization and Management of the "New Model" Pacification Program – 1966-1969* (RAND, 7 May, 1970), pp. 168, 257; R. W. Komer, 'Impact of Pacification on Insurgency in South Vietnam' (RAND, P-4443, August 1970), pp. 3, 5-6, 10.

3 General Galliéni, 'The Conquest of Madagascar' (1900) (*Rapport d'ensemble sur la pacification, l'organisation et la colonisation de Madagascar*), in Gérard Chaliand (ed.), *The Art of War in World History: From Antiquity to the Nuclear Age* (Berkeley, CA: University of California Press, 1994), pp. 813-5; Jean Gotmann, 'Bugeaud, Galliéni, Lyautney: The Development of French Colonial Warfare', in Edward Mead Earle (ed.), *Makers of Modern Strategy: Military Thought from Machiavelli to Hitler* (Princeton: Princeton University Press, 1943), pp. 243-4.

4 George Armstrong Kelly, *Lost Soldiers: The French Army and Empire in Crisis, 1947-1962* (Cambridge, MA: MIT Press, 1965), p. 93.

5 George A. Kelly, 'Revolutionary War and Psychological Action', *Military Review*, Vol. 40, No. 7, 1960, pp. 4-12, p. 12.

6 Roger Trinquier, *Modern Warfare* (1961), trans. Daniel Lee (Westport, CN: Praeger Security International 2006), p. 5.

7 David Galula, 'Notes on Pacification in Greater Kabylia' (1956), in David Gallula, *Pacification in Algeria, 1956-1958* (1963), (Santa Monica, CA: RAND, 2006), p. 269.

8 Galula, *Pacification in Algeria*, pp. 64-5.

9 David Galula, *Counterinsurgency Warfare: Theory and Practice* (1964), (Westport, CT: Praeger, 2006).

10 Bernd Greiner, *War Without Fronts: The USA in Vietnam* (2007), trans. Anne Wyburd and Victoria Fern (London: Bodley Head, 2009), p. 60.

11 William Gibson, *The Perfect War: Technowar in Vietnam* (New York: Grove Books, 1986), p. 281.

12 Johnson, to his advisors, cited in Frank L. Jones, 'Blowtorch: Robert Komer and the Making of Vietnam Pacification Policy', *Parameters: US Army War College Quarterly*, Vol. 35, No. 3, 2005, 103-118, p. 104; Komer, *Organization and Management*, p. 120.

13   Samuel L. Popkin, 'Pacification: Politics and the Village', *Asian Survey*, Vol. 10, No. 8, 1970, pp. 662-3.
14   Colonel Erwin R. Brigham, *Pacification Measurement in Vietnam: The Hamlet Evaluation System*, paper prepared for an Internal Security Seminar, Manila, 3-10 June, 1968, pp. 4-5, 10-12, 16, 19, 23. Brigham was Chief of the Research and Analysis Division of CORDS in Vietnam.
15   Geoffrey Fairbairn, *Revolutionary Guerrilla Warfare: The Countryside Version* (Harmondsworth: Penguin, 1974), pp. 239, 240.
16   Gibson, *Perfect War*, pp. 290-1, 299.
17   Kurt Jacobsen, *Pacification and Its Discontents* (Chicago: Prickly Paradigm Press, 2009), p. 87.
18   Gabriel Kolko, *Vietnam: Anatomy of War 1940-1975*,(London: Allen and Unwin, 1986), p. 236.
19   Cited in Gibson, *Perfect War*, p. 313.
20   Geoffrey Parker, *The Military Revolution: Military Innovation and the Rise of the West* (Cambridge: Cambridge University Press, 1996), p. 120.
21   Bernardo de Vargas Machuca, *Milicia Indiana* (1599), trans. Timothy F. Johnson, in Captain Bernardo de Vargas Machuca, *The Indian Militia and Description of the Indies* (Durham: Duke University Press, 2008), pp. 7, 26, 56, 77, 111, 116, 148.
22   Machuca, *Milicia Indiana*, pp. 148, 155-8; Bernardo de Machuca, *Defense and Discourse of the Western Conquests* (1603), trans. Timothy F. Johnson, in *Defending the Conquest: Bernardo de Machuca's Defense and Discourse of the Western Conquests*, ed. Kris Lane (University Park, PA: Pennsylvania State University Press, 2010), pp. 33, 40, 87, 89, 113, 114, 133, 134.
23   Cited in Tzvetan Todorov, *The Conquest of America* (New York: HarperPerennial, 1984), p. 173.
24   Cited in Todorov, *Conquest*, pp. 173-4.
25   Max Weber, *Economy and Society*, ed. Guenther Roth and Claus Wittich (California: University of California Press, 1978), pp. 972, 981.
26   Norbert Elias, *The Germans: Power Struggles and the Development of Habitus in the Nineteenth and Twentieth Centuries* (1989), trans. Eric Dunning and Stephen Mennell (New York: Columbia University Press, 1996), pp. 174, 176.
27   Peter B. Kraska, 'Crime Control as Warfare: Language Matters', in Peter B. Kraska (ed.), *Militarizing the American Criminal Justice System:*

The Changing Roles of the Armed Forces and the Police (Boston: Northeastern University Press, 2001); Dawn Moore and Kevin Haggerty, 'Bring It On Home: Home Drug Testing and the Relocation of the War on Drugs', *Social and Legal Studies*, Vol. 10, No. 3, 2001, pp. 377-95; Heinz Steinart, 'The Indispensable Metaphor of War: On Populist Politics and the Contradictions of the State's Monopoly of Force', *Theoretical Criminology*, Vol. 7, No. 3, 2003, pp. 265-91; Vincent Ruggiero, 'Criminalizing War: Criminology as Ceasefire', *Social and Legal Studies*, Vol. 14, No. 2, 2005, pp. 239-57.

28 Doug Stokes, *America's Other War: Terrorizing Columbia* (London: Zed Books, 2005), p. 3.

29 Georges Monbiot, 'A War of Terror', *The Guardian*, 4 February, 2003.

30 Chris Hables Gray, *Postmodern War: The New Politics of Conflict* (New York: Guilford Press, 1997), pp. 31-2; Timothy J. Dunn, *The Militarization of the U.S.-Mexico Border 1978-1992: Low-Intensity Conflict Doctrine Comes Home* (Austin, Texas: CMAS Books, 1996).

31 David Campbell, *Writing Security: United States Foreign Policy and the Politics of Identity* (Manchester: Manchester University Press, 1992), p. 210; Michael T. Klare, 'The Interventionist Impulse: U.S. Military Doctrine for Low-intensity Warfare', in Michael T. Klare and Peter Kornbluh (eds), *Low-Intensity Warfare: Counterinsurgency, Proinsurgency, and Antiterrorism in the Eighties* (New York: Pantheon Books, 1988), p. 72; Alfred W. McCoy, *The Politics of Heroin: CIA Complicity in the Global Drug Trade* (Chicago: Lawrence Hill Books, 2003), pp. 391-446; Jeremy Kuzmarov, *The Myth of the Addicted Army: Vietnam and the Modern war on Drugs* (Amherst: University of Massachusetts Press; 2009), pp. 103, 109; Michael Woodiwiss and David Bewly-Taylor, *The Global Fix: The Construction of a Global Enforcement Regime*, Transnational Institute, Amsterdam: TNI Briefing Series, No. 2005/3, 2005.

32 Loic Wacquant, *Punishing the Poor: The Neoliberal Government of Social Insecurity* (Durham: Duke University Press, 2009), pp. 61-2, 158; Nils Christie, *Crime Control as Industry* (London: Routledge, 1994), p. 69.

33 Michael Tonry, *Malign Neglect: Race, Crime, and Punishment in America* (Oxford: Oxford University Press, 1995), pp. 94, 104; Jerome G. Miller, *Search and Destroy: African-American Males in the Criminal Justice System* (Cambridge: Cambridge University Press, 1996), pp. 2, 83; Michael Sherry, *In the Shadow of War: The United States since the 1930s* (New Haven: Yale University Press, 1995), p. 450.

34 Herbert J. Gans, *The War Against the Poor: The Underclass and Antipoverty Policy* (New York: HarperCollins, 1995), p. 1.
35 S. R. Donziger, *The Real War on Crime: The Report of the National Criminal Justice Commission* (New York: HarperCollins, 1996), p. 218.
36 Marc Redfield, *The Rhetoric of Terror: Reflections on 9/11 and the War on Terror* (New York: Fordham University Press, 2009), p. 68.
37 Jacob Kipp, Lester Grau, Karl Prinslow and Captain Don Smith, 'The Human Terrain System: A CORDS for the 21st Century', *Military Review*, September-October, 2006, pp. 8-15.
38 Jennifer S. Light, *From Warfare to Welfare: Defense Intellectuals and Urban Problems in Cold War America* (Baltimore: Johns Hopkins University Press, 2003), p. 168.
39 House Un-American Activities Committee, *Guerrilla Warfare Advocates in the United States: Report by the Committee on Un-American Activities*, House Report No. 1351, 6 May, 1968 (Washington: US Government Printing Office, 1968), p. 62.
40 Robert Moss, *The War for the Cities* (New York: Coward, McCann and Geoghegan, 1972), p. 154. This connection was noted by Roberto J. Gonzalez, *Militarizing Culture: Essays on the Warfare State* (Walnut Creek, CA: Left Coast Press, 2010), pp. 113-4.
41 Frank Kitson, *Low Intensity Operations: Subversion, Insurgency, Peacekeeping* (London: Faber and Faber, 1971).

[2]

'To extend the scope of productive labour': Pacification as a police project.

GEORGE S. RIGAKOS

George W. Bush is gone and the war continues. Osama bin Laden is assassinated and the war continues. A war of police actions amidst economic collapse and imperial insurrection. A war against terror in the name of security. A global war. A war without end. A war that is everywhere and nowhere. Have we reached a critical moment? Are we now past the point of critically engaging with security? Are we fighting a losing analytic battle trying to re-define and reclaim security? If security has become the dominant, perhaps impenetrable concept of our times, then we must start entertaining the impossible. We must begin asking: what would doing *anti-*security look like? In this paper I begin to theoretically develop the concept of pacification for understanding two police projects: the formation of the Thames River Police of 1800 and the advent of Broken Windows policing in the 1990s. I treat these two case studies through the lens of pacification in order to provide examples of how critical scholars may re-imagine the hegemonic language of security, prioritize material considerations for understanding police power, and unearth existing relationships between domestic-imperial, military-civilian, war-peace, and public-private. It is in this sense that I hope to contribute to the larger analytic development of *anti-*security.

The problem of security

Security is not just hegemonic, it *is* hegemony. To be against security today is to stand against the entire global economic system. It seems almost unthinkable.

Even from a critical or social democratic perspective: how can anyone be against *social* security, *job* security, *personal* security, or *health* security? What about our *children's* security? How could anyone stand against *environmental* security? Anything in the name of security, therefore, appears as a greater good. Security was already the "supreme concept of bourgeoisie society"[1] as early as the 19th century but security after 9/11 has become all but unassailable. This is our problematic. The more security seems post-political, post-social, or even postmodern the more it escapes analytic scrutiny. The more security attaches itself to innumerable social relationships the more it becomes the very glue that binds social reality. Social problems become security problems. As security grafts itself onto almost every aspect of scientific endeavor it repositions the analysis in the form of some notion of governmentality[2] – not as a critique of governmentality but as an instrumental, pragmatic method of projecting liberal discourse over every sphere of that analysis.[3] There are now a litany of social issues being colonized by security, transforming them into analytic neologisms such as 'food security', 'supply-chain security', 'energy security' and so on… Each of these terms in their own way mask imperialist, exploitive and alienating objectives. Yet, on the face of it: what could be wrong with food security? Food security sounds like a noble endeavor, as do most security projects. But food security is being superimposed over a rather fundamental and communally solved dilemma: hunger. Food security presupposes a competition of interests. It presupposes a rational governmental discourse that alienates us from the rather basic human compulsion to simply feed the hungry. It also sets up a scenario of 'us versus them' and forces us to ask: whose food is it? How does sharing food increase or decrease *our* security? Because food is transformed into a security governance issue it is also sovereign issue, an issue of rational governmental discourse, a challenge of logistics and, by extension, a problem for liberalism. In short order, the communal and cultural compulsion to feed the hungry based on fellowship and love has been conceptually transformed into a liberal, technocratic problem based on competition and fear. This applies to almost all social problems mutated by the analytic appendage of security.

The ability for security to latch itself on to most aspects of human relations must therefore be recognized as an analytic and political blockage. Since there is no limit to the malleability and ubiquity of security and since security is roundly seen as something we should always want, the concept of security is not particularly useful for critical analyses. Even where there have been attempts by analysts of security to critique security or, (more likely) to critique *techniques* of security, the colossal security complex ends up consuming every critique as a method for its own improvement in the form of intelligence. The more security fails, the more it succeeds. Security breaches are met with security enhancements. Thus, we already know that security breeds insecurity but we should also understand that critiques of security also tend to broaden the analytic reach of security. Given this state of affairs, we are in dire need of developing a counter–hegemonic language in order to critically engage with the same substantive subject matter but from a heterodox political position. It is my assertion here that speaking of *pacification* or *projects of pacification* can excite our critical imagination in new ways. Pacification captures the mobilization of policing in a manner that sheds light on the objects, history and politics of such interventions. Thus, rather than obscuring global capitalist relations, pacification unpacks these connections.

Why pacification?

Pacification is not new but its proposed use as a critical concept for understanding police power certainly is. Its genealogy, as a project associated with the development of international relations as early as the sixteenth century, the control of colonial subjects, and as a euphemism for conquest and the suppression of resistance especially during the Vietnam War, has already been effectively developed by Neocleous.[4] We can now begin to interrogate the conceptual utility of pacification even further, not only as a critique of security but also forming the core of an analytic project for *anti-*security, as a new way for radical philosophies, sociologies, political economics and so forth to re-engage with the objects, politics and genealogies of security. The study of pacification promises to create such a space for radical inquiry because it seeks to: (1) problematize the objectives of security; (2) build analytic connections instead of masking them; (3) displace the ubiquity and reach of security; and anticipate (4) a state of war (including class war) viewing security as an active, unfinished project rife with resistance. Let's take a closer look at each of these four characteristics before considering two examples of pacification as projects of police.

Pacification problematizes the objectives of security. As I mentioned earlier, the concept of security has a generally positive connotation. Everybody wants to be secure. It could even be said that those that are insecure, that are in need of security, are being secured for their own good. That security is a civilizing project. Establishing security, therefore, is a good thing. And, of course, this is the problem for critical analysis. Security is like the roundly positive concept of community.[5] By attaching itself to otherwise coercive institutions and techniques these control practices seem more palatable: community policing, community corrections, community treatment, community watch, etc. But while we may want to be secure, do we really want to be pacified? Pacification thus presupposes resistance by subjects in ways that speaking of security simply does not – making the concept fertile ground for critical engagement. Pacification does not connote the roundly positive associations now inextricably bound up with the bourgeois concept of security. Indeed, it presupposes a very negative connotation.[6]

Pacification builds analytic connections instead of masking them. One of the problems of speaking about security is how easy it is to continuously divide security almost ad infinitum. The more you can divide and subdivide security the more security can colonize all aspects of human practices and thinking. It truly becomes, in the Marxist sense, 'the supreme concept of bourgeoisie society'. To a certain extent this has already been well documented by those who critically engage with security. That is, the interrelationship between domestic and international, civilian and military, public and private, etc. are false binaries that disguise far more than they reveal. What we find is that rather than policing domestically and conquering internationally, there is a presumption of a new continuous warfare that is both domestic and international. Looking at the history of security we see that these lineages can be better linked by speaking about pacification projects in the form of peace as warfare, or more precisely, that "civil society is always already at war"[7] – a long-standing attribute of capitalism to which I will return.

Pacification displaces the ubiquity and reach of security. While security is ubiquitous and can attach itself to almost any category of investigation, pacification simply cannot. For this reason alone it is a more worthwhile tool for critical inquiry. There is no such thing as food pacification, supply-chain pacification, private pacification, these ideas are nonsensical because pacification resists this type of ubiquity. Pacification forces us to ask: *who* is being pacified? *Why* are they being pacified and why are they resisting? *What* are the real objectives of this pacification project? You simply cannot ask the same questions in the same way when beginning from the language of security because security is more than an act it is an end-result, a goal, a feeling that imbues itself on all social relations and attaches itself to almost all commodities. Security hegemony casts a deep fog over police projects. A fog through which we may more effectively navigate by understanding pacification.

Pacification pre-supposes war and resistance. Pacification is a concept that is wedded to the presumption of war or at least an ongoing counter-insurgency against some sort of resistance. For this reason it uncovers what security seeks to mask: that the entire premise of security is based first and foremost on the security, extension and imposition of property relations and that these property relations are the manifestations of brute force both legislatively and through what we would call pacification, including but not limited to: enforcement of a wage-labor system, the expropriation of land, the removal of the opportunity for sustenance, the erasure of communal organization, the imposition of individual competition, the establishment of commodity culture and so forth. Pacification becomes largely transparent as a war footing to secure these objectives. Pacification, therefore, is not passive. Security pretends to be. To study pacification makes it clear that we are studying the fabrication of a social order.[8] The 'population' will never feel secure. Pacification does not presuppose security for its objects. It only presupposes their pacification for the purpose of rendering them productive. Thus, we can no longer ignore the political economy,[9] the global interconnectivity of pacification. Between June 26 and 27, 2010 the Canadian government spent close to 1 billion dollars on security measures for the G20 in Toronto, providing protection for the ceremonial gathering of global state and corporate elites. Mass arrests, illegal detentions, the secret enactment of wartime legislation banning persons from approaching public buildings or parks, and the deployment of over 20,000 police, military and intelligence personnel marked the largest 'peacetime' mobilization in Canadian history. A few months later, Egypt erupted into a mass revolt against the tyranny of Mubarak and western nations were slow, indeed reticent, to support the popular uprising. U.S. made tear gas canisters, the same used against protesters in Toronto, were fired into the Egyptian crowds in Tahrir Square. As the battle waged between security forces and the people in the streets, analysts began to describe the cozy relationship between Mubarak and U.S. Secretary of State Clinton and revealed that for over two decades, the Egyptian military had been receiving over 1 billion dollars in annual aid to support the regime. More and more the political economy, tactics, logics and even hardware of pacification seem part of the same domestic and global imperatives of Empire.[10] More and more, these tactics are obfuscated behind a series of rhetorical strategies of security. We must interrogate this larger political economy.

In the next two sections I offer two cases of pacification projects in the form of police initiatives: (1) the creation of the Thames River Police in 1800 and the early police thinking that preceded it, and (2) Broken Windows policing, a strategy that was first described in 1982 but became widely acclaimed and adopted by the end of the 1990s. These cases are almost 200 years apart, but they are indicative of an overall theme of pacification that runs across many historical and contemporary police initiatives. Most analysts of policing and security will immediately understand the significance of both the emergence of the Thames River police and the contemporary police strategy known as 'Broken Windows Policing'. In what is to follow, I rely on the pronouncements of each initiative's key architects. Their pronouncements reveal significant overlaps in both thinking and purpose, and each police project's intimate connection to capital.

Case 1: Petty, Colquhoun and The Thames River Police

The Thames River Police under the direction of the famous police intellectual and magistrate Patrick Colquhoun began to patrol the docks, quays and hulks of London's shipping artery in 1800. But over a century and a half before the emergence of this first privately financed, yet legislatively formalized, uniformed, salaried, commercial police, Sir William Petty was laying out the groundwork for a 'political arithmetic' that would help change Enlightenment thinking about governance. Petty has long been appreciated as the "founder of political economy" and the "inventor of statistics".[11] His *Natural and Political Observations on the Bills on Mortality* (attributed to John Graunt)[12] laid the foundation for a new system of governmentality that would significantly alter how sovereigns viewed their subjects through the prism of 'populations.' Thus, while Petty has been acknowledged for his revolutionary contribution to political economy he has received scant attention for his contribution to the development of 'police science.' He understood before most that the true source of wealth of the emerging capitalist system would come not from rent and property but through the circulation of 'free labour' which would be able to "superlucrate millions upon millions"[13] for the Kingdom. Marx, for example, recognized Petty's "audacious genius"[14] because he understood the mechanics of capital long before his contemporaries. Petty also personally benefitted from his statistical and analytical gifts as he was granted sizeable estates including the Irish town of Kenmar that he designed using triangular roadways bearing his name and title. He developed not only the broad project of political economy, but also understood that wealth creation was dependent on a systematic approach to surveillance and control of populations through accounting. He noted as early as 1690 in his advice to the Crown that the Irish simply refused to work more than the few hours necessary to secure their own sustenance. Since the Irish had access to land and because they were able to grow their own food this undermined the kingdom's ability to extract their full productive potential. His recommendations included forcibly "transporting them and their goods" so that the Irish would have little choice other than to sell their labour in the factories of England. The expropriation of their land, therefore, was part of a civilizing process that would make them closer to the English. Of course, more abundant wealth could be accrued by 'freeing' the Irish labourer creating: "... spare Hands enough among the King of England's Subjects, to earn two Millions per annum more than they now do; and that there are also Employments, ready, proper, and sufficient, for that purpose".[15]

Sir William Petty's abilities at surveying and urban planning were thus aimed at eliciting the maximum level of productivity from subjects of the English Crown, including those who lived in cities. Not only is this expressed in Petty's design of the Irish town of Kenmar but even more so in his detailed plan for the city of London including especially the erection of an encircling wall. He argued that this 'London wall' should be "100m foot in circumference, 11 foot-high, two brick thick, in a fortification figure, with 20 gates, worth 20m£..." But what would the purpose of such a wall be? For the security of the city? In part, but this seems only supplementary to its primary function for Petty. Thus, the function of the wall was "[t]o take an accompt of all persons and things going in and out of the Citty" and to provide "[a] foundation of libertyes, securityes, and priviledges" which included who may be allowed into the city, how their possessions should be catalogued, a taxation system, a system of management for those who were not productive, a licensing system for beggars and so forth. William Petty's London wall is an architectural design that goes far beyond bricks and mortar. For the first time in recorded history a city wall was to be erected not for the purposes of fortification and defense but rather as a method of surveillance and for the best means of keeping accounts. The gates would be guarded not by sword but by pen.[16] Metaphorically, therefore, the London wall symbolizes the confluence of the project of police and capital through the statistical ordering of populations, the end purpose of which was to make subjects more 'productive'. Years earlier, Petty imagined a much more austere system for delinquents and debtors in Ireland, including that "all men be bound to keep Accompts of their Receipts and Issues, Gayn and Losse, Debts & Credits, in mony, Cattle & Goods, and where they were at noon and every night every day in the yeare, with mention of what deeds here hath made or witnessed". No house would stand alone nor outside the call of some other house in order to ensure effective communication in times of crisis and to allow for a system of surveillance and apprehension. Finally, Petty proposed in the middle of the 17th century what has now become a common refrain among the security establishment: a national identification system so that "[every] man carry about him an uncounterfitable Tickett, expressing his name, the numero of his Howse, his Age, Trade, Stature, Haire, eye, and other peculiar marks of his Body."[17] Thus, not only was Sir William Petty the inventor of statistics, the founder of political economy, and early colonial surveyor and planner, he was also one of the initial architects of capitalism by arguing for the establishment and enforcement of a wage labor system. He thus laid the groundwork for the development of 'police science' to follow, very early recognizing not only that the new source of wealth under capitalist relationships would be 'free labour' but simultaneously understanding the forms of surveillance and pacification necessary to make capitalism function.

While Petty is often recognized for his contribution to political economy yet largely unappreciated for his contribution to police science,[18] the reverse is true of Patrick Colquhoun. Long recognized as the strongest proponent of the 'new police' that would eventually patrol the streets of London in 1830, most police analysts overlook his important contribution to political economy. Before Colquhoun was to become famous for advocating a London police that was centralized, salaried, and professional he was a commercial master in the New England colony of Virginia, specializing in shipping and trade. As a loyalist to the Crown he also helped finance a Glasgow Regiment sent to put down the emerging American revolution. Thus, before Colquhoun penned his famous *Treatise On The Commerce and Police of the River Thames*[19] and his opus *Treatise on the Police of the Metropolis*[20] he was compiling one of the most comprehensive statistical overviews of the resources of the British empire. Like Sir William Petty before him, Colquhoun understood in his catalogue of the British Empire's holdings that "[the] resources of nations are derived from the productive labour of the people" and that this labour "is augmented or diminished according to forms of government, and the intelligence, ability and zeal... in those to whom it is assigned to direct the state of affairs of states and empires".[21] Petty experimented with the Irish, Colquhoun with the Virginians. Both, however, subsequently proposed policing projects *domestically*, aimed at the 'indigent poor', the criminal classes and eventually the entire English working class.

Of course, the police role in the class-based functioning of economic prosperity can hardly be overlooked. The logic used by Colquhoun was utilitarian; the port of London stood to loose upwards of 60 million pounds, whereas the cost of maintaining his police force amounted to only a fraction of that cost. Likewise, his conception of police extended 'security to Commercial Property', where he claimed that "the privileges of innocence will be preserved, and the comforts of Civil society eminently enlarged".[22] Colquhoun clearly realized that social control then was geared to the benefit of a particular class of property holders, which was consistent with his emphasis on managing the various classes of persons who he said threatened commercial interests. This class politics was especially obvious in his work for the Thames shippers and London merchants where he set about instituting a system of surveillance that eliminated customary compensation outside official lumping rates (wages). He argued for "the abolition of the perquisite of chips", including "sweepings", "samplings"[23] and "the abolition of fees and perquisites of every description" in favour of "a liberal increase in salaries".[24] This form of cost rationalization is thus a harbinger of Fordism to come over a century later. A predictable system of compensation had to be enforced in order to guarantee profits. This meant that pre-capitalist customs such as taking the fruits of what one has worked on with one's hands had to be eliminated as a practice. Of course, Colquhoun's initiatives did not go unopposed. The Thames River police office was soon attacked and almost burnt down by rioting workers. But Colquhoun persisted and, in the long run, was able to boast that his new system of police had saved the river's commercial interests over 122£ million.

Colquhoun skillfully created and enforced a wage labour system at the precise time and place where international capitalism demanded it most – the heart of Imperial England. The lumping rates were arrived at so that "honest labour can be procured for daily wages" and so that lumpers would not resort to 'plunder'.[25] Rates were publicly posted at the Thames Police office. Master lumpers (dock foremen) were scrutinized by the police; clothing used to conceal customs and payments in kind such as wide trousers, jemmies, and concealed pockets were banned; lumpers were searched; all ships, contents and manifests registered and their contents guarded. Colquhoun's 'police machine'[26] was directed specifically at class discipline by uplifting the indigent poor and fabricating the working conditions of the 'useful' poor. He believed that "by this... a confidence is to be established... the improvement of public morals will contribute, in an eminent degree, to the happiness and prosperity of the country".[27] The purpose of this police machine was clear: "to extend the scope of productive labour"[28] if not directly in the production of goods then certainly in intensifying exploitation in the circuit of capital through the transport of commodities at the docks.[29]

Case 2: Broken Windows

Broken Windows policing is perhaps the most widely recognized criminal justice initiative of the past 30 years. First presented as a policing program utilizing foot patrol and aimed at pushing back against criminality in inner-city neighborhoods, the Broken Windows 'philosophy'[30] is now considered the most 'common-sense' approach for responding to urban crime and has been adopted by police departments across North America. First articulated by James Q. Wilson and George Kelling in a 1982 issue of *Atlantic Monthly*, the Broken Windows approach seeks to take minor incivilities and low-level offenses seriously. The authors argue that decriminalizing disreputable behavior that supposedly harms no one and thus removing "the ultimate sanction the police can employ to maintain neighborhood order" is "a mistake". While, "[a]rresting a single drunk or a single vagrant who has harmed no identifiable person seems unjust... failing to do anything about a score of drunks or a hundred vagrants may destroy an entire community". Kelling and Wilson advocate consistent and persistent proactive policing aimed at putting a lid on the antisocial behavior that forces respectable neighborhood citizens off the city streets. By empowering police to move drunks to the back of the alley, stop gang members from catcalling, and generally to move vagrants and undesirables away from areas where people congregate, meet, and shop the authors believe that a 'domino effect' can be averted so that the neighborhood does not become abandoned to a criminal element whose deviant behavior escalates over time. In short, according to Broken Windows, preventing minor public incivilities and low-level offenses today will directly prevent more serious offenses from occurring in the future.

Were it not for the adoption of the Broken Windows approach by the New York City Police Department in the 1990s under the direction of chief William Bratton and Mayor Rudolph Giuliani the program may very well have been relegated to the dustbin of history. The Broken Windows approach was being rhetorically trumped by very similar "community-based policing",[31] "problem oriented policing",[32] "intelligence led policing"[33] and other policing deployment strategies based on "crime mapping"[34] and a general movement toward foot patrol programs in commercial corridors. The stories of the success of the Broken Windows approach in New York City are now legendary amongst executives, policymakers, and criminal justice practitioners involved in policing. The approach involved manifold changes to the direction of police provision in New York City that included: (1) scrubbing clean subway cars to eliminate graffiti or any appearance of disorder; (2) sanitizing street facades and immediately tending to maintenance concerns such as faulty lighting, graffiti and other signs of disrepair; (3) a massive redeployment of foot patrol in commercial sectors across the city; (4) the implementation of a system of accountability among precinct commanders aimed at reducing crime, reducing fear and increasing satisfaction toward the NYPD known as COMPSTAT; (5) the relentless pursuit of homeless persons and the enactment of special state legislation aimed at empowering police to target populations engaged in illicit street commerce such as squeegee kids and panhandlers; and (6) the creation of special enforcement squads that would stalk recently released or paroled inmates in an attempt to catch them in the act of engaging in minor offenses for re-arrest.

The success story of Broken Windows in the 1990s elevated both Bratton and Giuliani to almost mythic crime fighting status. They were heroes for returning order to Gotham.[35] The statistical decline in violent crime in New York City was indeed dramatic[36] as was the visual 'cleanup' of Manhattan, especially in Times Square. In the late-eighteenth century, Patrick Colquhoun would cautiously draw back the curtains of his horse-drawn carriage to count up the number of prostitutes and vagabonds on the streets of London in order to offer evidence of the need for a new police.

Over 200 years later, in the early morning hours Giuliani would similarly scan the streets of New York City from the back of his Mayoral limousine dictating cleanup orders to his staff. Soon after, NYPD paddy wagons would round up "suitable enemies",[37] by-laws would be introduced to shut down peep shows, graffiti would be removed and the bustle of sidewalk shell games and illicit dealings silenced. Yet, by September 11, 2001 Giuliani's star had begun to fade. Broken Windows had become conflated with 'zero tolerance' and a 'cowboy culture' had permeated the NYPD resulting in repeated cases of police brutality that were traced back to Giuliani's get tough tactics in the popular imagination.[38] While Giuliani had become less popular, Broken Windows was being exported as a policing philosophy throughout North America and the world. Giuliani's management of the aftermath of the terrorist attack on New York City would once again vault him into national consciousness making him a viable Republican presidential candidate in 2008. The connection between domestic policing and international terror became embodied in Giuliani's candidacy and in his subsequent venture as a security consultant and public speaker.

When his appointed security protégé, former bodyguard and business associate Bernard Kruk was disqualified as the next Homeland Security Director by Congress, Kruk was then selected by Secretary of Defense Donald Rumsfeld to form a new domestic police force in Iraq. He quickly set about implementing a Broken Windows philosophy in Baghdad as the de facto chief of the Iraqi National Police.[39] Broken Windows philosophy thus became exported as an international police tactic to pacify Baghdad. For Kruk, the connections between terrorist attacks and minor crimes in Baghdad were as direct as they were between homicides and minor antisocial behaviour in New York City. His mentor, Rudy Giuliani argued as much in *Foreign Affairs*:[40] "When security is reliably established in a troubled part of a city, normal life rapidly reestablishes itself: shops open, people move back in, children start playing ball on the sidewalks again, and soon a decent and law-abiding community returns to life". "The same is true in world affairs", he continues. "Disorder in the world's bad neighbourhoods tends to spread. Tolerating bad behaviour breeds more bad behaviour". Broken Windows had thus gone from neighbourhood reclamation project to geopolitical stabilization tactic with little critical reflection.

The Iraqi provisional government, under the direction of a U.S.-led capitalist "shock doctrine"[41] had already implemented a mass neoliberal selloff of its assets, privatized its key resources, destroyed organized labor, and generally opened itself up to international plunder. Now, under the auspices of continuing to make itself 'open for business', a motto shared with urban policing initiatives throughout the world, the Authority imported a policing pacification project for this new "human terrain."[42] US military strategists adopted Broken Windows under the questionable assumption that Baghdad in 2006 was comparable to New York City in the 1980s. The School of Advanced Military Studies claimed that "[a]lthough different in scope and scale, the conditions in Iraq today are comparable to those that existed in pre-1994 New York

City" because "[t]he country is inundated with firearms and explosives which are used in a continuous cycle of violence in order to achieve political, religious or criminal objectives".[43] The document's author then argues for "applying the NYPD crime control model to restore public order in Iraq". COMPSTAT was replaced by TERRORSTAT, foot patrol with patrols in force behind armored Humvees, and Kruk, now nicknamed the 'Baghdad Terminator' set about reducing terrorist attacks by raiding brothels and cracking down on minor drug dealers with predictably dismal results.

It is tempting to focus on the rather questionable logic of attempting to transform what is, in essence, a concentrated foot patrol program designed to tame inner-city disorder into a police counterinsurgency program for urban environments rife with internecine religious war, anti-western jihadism and suicide bombers. Perhaps this is too obvious a critique. What might not be as obvious, however, is the ease with which a domestic policing program found a relatively similar operational logic in the midst of an occupational campaign aimed at advancing American imperial interests through pacification. It begs the question: if the proponents of these policing strategies are arguing for their tactical interchangeability in either ostensibly democratic, peaceful, domestic urban environments or stateless, war-torn, overseas markets then shouldn't we begin to look more carefully at what is being guaranteed under the name of security for making places and people more productive?[44] Especially when one considers that under the auspices of Broken Windows and zero tolerance policing in cities such as Fresno California, 40-unit SWAT teams disembark from armoured personnel carriers in 'urban tactical gear' and armed with assault rifles to 'suppress' an 'inner-city war zone'. As one tactical team member put it: "[w]hen the soldiers ride in, you should see those blacks scatter".[45] One need only cut to a 'patrol in force' by U.S. Marines in central Baghdad for strikingly similar imagery. Broken Windows has thus rhetorically morphed from its original formulation some three decades ago. Today, it is used as a code word for an aggressive, 'zero tolerance' approach to establish security. It seeks to civilize not only inner-city black youth but also unproductive Arabs. This form of authoritarian neoliberalism has very deep roots and it is interwoven with the very fabric of capital accumulation and the creation of wage labour and viable systems of consumption. We must start taking account of this lineage, this genealogy, and the often predictable trajectories of both the discourse and tactics in which they occur by situating these approaches within larger political processes of pacification.

Studying Pacification Projects

There is certainly far more to be said about either the early formation of a science of police or contemporary police tactics as potential sources of study through the lens of pacification than my skeletal observations allow. But what I hope I have demonstrated here is the conceptual utility of pacification for analyzing the broad vision of police and capital, both in the operating logic and political economy that subtended the creation of the first bona fide, centralized, salaried, professional police and the contemporary project of Broken Windows. There are many other examples that have similar orientations and ends, rooted in similar principles of expanding capital and creating docile bodies for economic exploitation. By summarizing the connections between the Thames River Police and Broken Windows approach I aim to provide a start for a broader investigation of police pacification projects. These similarities may be summarized as follows: First, both projects have *imperial objectives.* The techniques, technologies and objectives are similar with respect to the continuity of pacification of either domestic populations or the exploitation of overseas subjects. Both Broken Windows and the Thames Police are legitimized on the basis of: (1) making labour more 'productive' within the international circuit of capital, (2) fabricating a system that privileges the global protection of private property, and (3) establishing a circuit of cosmopolitan consumption by making urban spaces 'open for business' and thus ripe for economic exploitation. Second, both *employ police networks.* Thus, in both of these cases a wide network of public, private and quasi-public institutions[46] are employed to achieve the same ends marshaling the resources of the private sector and the military in order to assist in the extraction of resources, the control of the populations, and the overall creation of productive relations. Third, both are offered as *civilizing initiatives.* Whether domestically or in foreign territory, 'police actions' are civilizing interventions.[47] In both of these cases there is even a sense of restoration; the restoration of order in particular. Alongside this is a project of education in order that the population may buy into the system. Today, we call this 'hearts and minds' in Afghanistan and Iraq. In the past, it was making colonial subjects 'more like the English' in Ireland and India. Fourth, both are *covers for war* that anticipate *resistance* or insurgency. The rhetoric of obtaining a peace or a sense of security is actually to acknowledge an already existing state of war. This may be low intensity domestic warfare, precision military strikes, or even international police actions.

The need to pacify spaces and people whether under the metaphor of 'a war on crime' or whether through acts like 'patrols in force' are, in effect, covers for class warfare. The use of force to separate people from the land, to fabricate a social order based on the wage-labour system, and to inculcate a neo-liberal system through the threat of force all under the rubric of security – these are projects of police that may be understood as part of the long durée[48] of pacification under capitalist relations.

Notes

1. Karl Marx, *A Contribution to the Critique of Political Economy* (Chicago: C.H. Kerr, 1904).
2. Michel Foucault, 'Governmentality', in Graham Burchell, Colin Gordon and Peter Miller (eds), *The Foucault Effect: Studies in Governmentality*, (Chicago: University of Chicago Press, 1991).
3. George S. Rigakos and Richard W. Hadden, 'Crime, Capitalism and the Risk Society: Towards the Same Olde Modernity?', *Theoretical Criminology*, Vol. 5, No. 1, 2001, pp. 61-84.
4. Mark Neocleous, 'War as Peace, Peace as Pacification', *Radical Philosophy* 159, 2010, pp. 8-17; Neocleous, this volume.
5. Carl Klockars, 'The Rhetoric of of Community Policing', in Jack Greene and Stephen Mastrofski (eds), *Community Policing: Rhetoric or Reality* (New York: Praeger, 1988).
6. Except, perhaps, in consoling crying babies.
7. Neocleous, 'War as Peace', p. 16.
8. Mark Neocleous, *The Fabrication of Social Order: A Critical Theory of Police Power* (London: Pluto Press, 2000).
9. Steven Spitzer, 'The Political Economy of Policing', in David F. Greenberg (ed.), *Crime and Capitalism: Readings in Marxist Criminology* (Palo Alto: Mayfield, 1981).
10. Michael Hardt and Antonio Negri, *Empire* (Cambridge MA: Harvard University Press, 2001).
11. See the pronouncements made by the Marquis of Lansdowne in Sir William Petty, *The Petty Papers: Some Unpublished Writings (Vol. 1)*, ed. Marquis of Lansdowne, vol. 1, 2 vols. (London: Constable, 1927).
12. John Graunt (and Sir William Petty), *Natural and Political Observations Mentioned in a Following Index, and Made Upon the Bills of Mortality* (London: Tho: Roycroft, for John Martin, James Allestry, and Tho: Dicas, at the Sign of the Bell in St. Paul's Church-yard, 1662).
13. See J. Brewer, 'Law and Disorder in Stuart and Hanoverian England', *History Today*, January 1980, pp. 18-27.
14. Marx, *Contribution to the Critique of Political Economy*. App. A fn.2.
15. Petty, *The Petty Papers: Some Unpublished Writings (Vol. 1)* iv.
16. Juri Mykkänen, '"To Methodize and Regulate Them": William Petty's Governmental Science of Statistics', *History of the Human Sciences*, 7, 1994, pp. 65-88.
17. Petty, *The Petty Papers: Some Unpublished Writings (Vol. 1)* Nos. 10 to 17.

18 except see Rigakos and Hadden, 'Crime, Capitalism and the Risk Society'.
19 Patrick Colquhoun, *Treatise on the Commerce and Police of the River Thames* (London: Baldwin and Son, 1800).
20 Patrick Colquhoun, *Treatise on the Police of the Metropolis, Etc.* (London: Mawman, 1800).
21 Patrick Colquhoun, *A Treatise on the Wealth, Power, and Resources of the British Empire* (London: Joseph Mawman, 1814), p. 49.
22 Patrick Colquhoun, *A Treatise on the Commerce and Police of the River Thames* (London: Joseph Mawman, 1800), p. 38.
23 Colquhoun, *Treatise on the Commerce and Police of the River Thames*, p. 138.
24 Colquhoun, *Treatise on the Police of the Metropolis, Etc.*, p. 355.
25 Colquhoun, *Treatise on the Commerce and Police of the River Thames*, p. 619.
26 John L. McMullan, 'Social Surveillance and the Rise of the "Police Machine"', *Theoretical Criminology*, Vol. 2, No. 1, 1998, pp. 93-117.
27 Colquhoun, *Treatise on the Commerce and Police of the River Thames*.
28 Colquhoun, *Treatise on the Wealth, Power, and Resources*, p. 232.
29 For Marx, the system of distribution falls under Department II which means that no surplus value is realized at the point of sale since no additional value has been added by the retailer. Nonetheless, the transport industry was an exception to this for Marx as the movement of goods which included the expenditure of resources and labour to make commodities available for consumption certainly added to the exchange value of goods, making those working in the transport industry "productive."
30 James Q. Wilson and George L. Kelling, 'Broken Windows: The Police and Neighbourhood Safety', *Atlantic Monthly*, March 1982, pp. 29-38.
31 Robert Trojanowicz and B. Bucqueroux, *Community Policing: A Contemporary Perspective* (Cincinnati: Anderson Publishing, 1990).
32 H. Goldstein, *Problem-Oriented Policing* (New York: McGraw-Hill, 1990).
33 Marilyn Peterson, *Intelligence-Led Policing: The New Intelligence Architecture*. (Washington: Bureau of Justice Assistance, 2005).
34 P.J. Brantingham and P.L. Brantingham, eds., *Environmental Criminology* (Beverly Hills: Sage, 1981).
35 Peter K. Manning, 'Theorizing Policing: The Drama and Myth of

Crime Control in the NYPD', *Theoretical Criminology*, Vol. 5, No. 3, 2001, pp. 315-344.
36   George L. Kelling and Catherine Coles, *Fixing Broken Windows: Restoring Order and Reducing Crime in Our Communities* (New York: Free Press, 1996).
37   Nils Christie, 'Suitable Enemies', in H. Bianchi and R. Van Swaaningen (eds), *Abolitionism: Toward a Non-Repressive Approach to Crime* (Amsterdam: Free University Press, 1986).
38   Police brutality against Abner Louima in 1997 and the shooting death of Amadou Diallo in 1999 were particularly damaging to Giuliani's reputation.
39   Christie, 'Suitable Enemies'.
40   Rudolph Giuliani, 'Toward a Realistic Peace: Defending Civilization and Defeating Terrorists by Making the International System Work', *Foreign Affairs*, Vol. 86, No. 5, 2007, pp. 2-18.
41   Naomi Klein, *The Shock Doctrine: The Rise of Disaster Capitalism* (Toronto: Vintage Books, 2008).
42   See: http://humanterrainsystem.army.mil/ (Accessed May 25, 2011)
43   Robert E. Gordon, *The Iraqi Police Service and Compstat: Applying the Nypd Crime Control Model to Restore Public Order in Iraq* (Forth Leavenworth), p. iii.
44   Or, I should say *representationally* productive in the sense that subjects of pacification are being rendered as consumers and the urban spaces they traverse as untapped *markets* in need of exploitation in the circuit of capital.
45   Peter B. Kraska and Victor E. Kappeler, 'Militarizing American Police: The Rise and Normalization of Police Paramilitary Units', *Social Problems*, Vol. 44, No. 1, 1997, pp. 1-18, p. 10.
46   Kraska and Kappeler, 'Militarizing American Police', p. 10.
47   Kraska and Kappeler, 'Militarizing American Police., p. 10.
48   Fernand Braudel, *Capitalism and Material Life 1400-1800*, trans. George Weidenfeld and Nicolson Ltd. (New York: Harper and Row, 1973).

[3]

Public Policing, Private Security, Pacifying Populations

MICHAEL_KEMPA

In this chapter, I challenge the conventional wisdom that the resurgent private security industry amounts to a threat to the public interest that is best dealt with through more active state-led regulation (i.e., 'democratic anchoring') and increased public policing to serve the collective interest. This is because the both public and private policing have common historical origins, and, more deeply, are linked to the same political economy: both sets of modern security agencies work in common towards the pacification of populations in service of the growth of markets and thus the interests of capital. As such, a pro-social means of 'security' is no more likely to be seated in the public than the private realm: what is at issue is the discovery and promotion of a social order organized around human need rather than political security; in transcending the limits of capitalist security, this project falls outside the question of the public or the private. The key to this project, therefore, lies not in regulating or somehow democratically anchoring existing security regimes of either a public or private nature; rather, it lies in finding and supporting the spread of a social solidarity that is different in substance from contemporary capitalist security.[1]

To develop these arguments, this chapter begins with a review of developments in private policing, and surveys the social and democratic dangers that these trends have been considered to pose. It then discusses the limitations of existing proposals for ways of dealing with these challenges through principally state mechanisms. These limitations, suggest that thinking critically about the ways in which policing supports capital will hopefully create the conceptual space necessary for the consideration, and gradual experiment-led implementation, of a politics that transcends security; that looks to human emancipation rather than pacification.

The resurgence of private authority

Whatever monopoly that the public police may once have held over the business of collective security, those days have passed. Over the last three or four decades, private security has grown exponentially in both the 'established' democracies of the West and the fledgling democracies of the 'post-authoritarian' and more generally 'developing' world. Pioneering research in the 1970s and 1980s that first drew scholarly attention to this trend[2] gave a lead that has been taken up with increasing vigour in academic policing studies over the past few years. Particular focal points in empirical analysis have been the massive overall size of the private security industry (which dwarfs public policing, by any measure of analysis),[3] the broad range of functions that the industry seeks to engage,[4] and the forms of repressive and seductive modalities of power the industry relies upon to effect these purposes.[5] Further, political economic histories of policing reveal that a private security apparatus that dwarfs public policing in terms of sheer size, activity, and social impact is the historical norm: as we shall develop, public policing emerged following the example of corporate security, and the latter has outshadowed the former throughout modern western history, apart from a very brief period over the middle decades of the 20th century, which were characterised by welfare liberal politics.[6]

There are currently no functions performed by public policing agencies that are also not somewhere and sometimes performed by private security actors.[7] This is true at the local level of generic crime control activities and is equally true with respect to macro-level 'national security' issues. On the local scale, private security is involved in securing fortified forms of communal space which are privately owned yet open in various degrees to public access. Such new forms of communal space have come to dominate the contemporary urban and rural landscape, with the effect that more and more social activity takes place on private, corporatised space, governed according to the dictates of capital.[8]

At the macro-level, large security corporations are involved in collaborating with states to secure national borders. They are heavily involved in military adventures in Iraq, Afghanistan, Asia-Pacific, and throughout the continents of Africa and South America. Notably, in Iraq, private armies are so heavily involved as to stand as the second largest contingent in the 'Coalition of the Willing' – a participant army smaller than only that of the United States, and larger than that of Britain or Australia. Further, if not somewhat ironically, in post-war, 'transitional' democratic contexts, private security firms are often contracted by states to carry out public police training.[9]

At all levels of engagement, private security companies promote their clients' interests first, ahead of more broadly public interests, with the emphasis most frequently placed on preventing and reducing loss or damage at private sites rather than on apprehending and punishing those who violate the law or promoting peace beyond the frontiers of their enclaves of privilege.[10] As such, when not acting in a straight-forward military (and thus sovereign) capacity, private security agencies tend most often to produce a type of risk-oriented order that seeks to eliminate the possibility of problems and breaches of security happening in advance of their occurrence.

Key to concerns regarding the impacts of this industry is the fact that much of this preventive order centres around promoting the interests of capitalist paymasters, who require pacific and docile bodies to consume the maximum possible number and amount of the goods and services that are on offer for sale in today's consumptive new communal spaces of work and leisure. As such, non-criminal behaviours that are simply disruptive to profit-making are the targets of exclusionary regimes of disciplinary surveillance, as all manner of corporate spaces – ranging from the shopping centre to the university campus – are policed according to the dictates of consumption.

Following along from this, academics, and, in some cases, practitioners, have been concerned with the social and cultural impacts of exclusionary private security practices, in terms of: the reduction in quality of the experience of citizenship on the part of economically marginalized segments of the community; negative impacts upon the development and expression of individual and collective identity; personal feelings of lack of safety; and the straight-forward abuse of constitutional rights and personal liberties by private authorities that are not constrained in the same fashion as state actors by constitutional law and charter/bill of rights protections.[11]

Such a focus on the pacification of the denizens of corporatised, communal space is often contrasted with the assumed reactive nature of public policing agencies, who are largely frustrated in their efforts to be proactive (i.e., 'intrusive') by the restraints of constitutional protections of the individual right not to be harassed by public authority on the basis of unfounded, generalised suspicion. For many authors, the solution to dealing with the above problems has thereby been to suggest that the state itself must lead the charge towards re-democratizing policing, order, and human security generally within contemporary society.

Perhaps the most well-developed work in this regard has been that produced by Ian Loader and Neil Walker.[12] For these authors, there is a default, large and long-term role for the state in coordinating public-private networks for security on the basis that the state taking the lead in these processes will perform a certain 'civilizing' function: it is hypothesized that members of the public will be responsibilised to turn away from esoteric, private, corporatised interests to engage security in pro-democratic (and more broadly pro-social) and inclusive terms under the watchful eye, and with the encouragement, of the state. While these authors do consider that private security may make a useful contribution to collective order, they charge that there is a default, and dominant role for the state to play in mobilising and coordinating state-private partnerships for public order and security.

That the state is supposed, in all cases and as a matter of democratic principle, to be charged with the responsibility to steer security programs in the direction of the public interest is a puzzling argument on a number of levels. While it may be the case that certain state agencies may have such a role in particular sets of circumstances, we will develop the argument that it is more useful to take this as a question or possibility to be considered on an evidence-based, case by case basis, rather than as an article of faith: an openness to the possibility of valuable state contribution to collective order is best tempered by hearty state skepticism for two interrelated sets of reasons.

First off, a fair amount of criminological, sociological and political work over decades of critical enquiry has pointed to a whole manner of issues, problems and contradictions concerning the public police and the state criminal justice system more broadly. It seems peculiar that these same public agencies, whose contribution to collective order has been so roundly criticized, are now conceived as being the a-priori solution to the apparently greater problem of the contribution of private security and order to collective life. If we consider that the private security industry is guilty of all manner of abuses of personal liberties, the perversion of social justice, the transformation of social space in the image of capital, and overall pacification of human beings in the model of docile producers and consumers, what of the decades of critical evidence that indicts public policing in exactly the same terms? What of the near century of violent strike-breaking, labour union disruption, and, more latterly, crushing of social and economic protest (even where peaceable) by the police in direct service of corporate power and, at other times, state government, on both sides of the Atlantic in Britain and North America?[13] What of the very many thousands of known abuses of ethnic minorities, the poor, those considered to be sexually deviant, women, and the mentally ill through the unjustified application of repressive sovereign power and targeted disciplinary surveillance (i.e., 'profiling') by the public police? And these very many terrible things have taken place under the watchful eye of the elaborate and expensive system for 'democratic anchoring/accountability' for public policing that the state has constructed - and constantly revisited and tinkered with over the course of five decades - at the behest of the well-intentioned left?[14] Are we to assume that such abuses will simply vanish in the face of the need to re-consolidate ultimate responsibility for the policing function in public hands to quash the 'greater threat' of the historically-normal return to dominance of corporate security?

The second, and related reason for which a re-publicisation of collective security to serve social interests is a false hope, is that public and private security share more institutional, technological and practical characteristics than separate them. This commonality of characteristics can be traced directly to the common political economic heritage that underpins both public and private institutions for liberal capitalist security. As already intimated above, modern public policing, as we know it, traces its institutional heritage to experiments in the corporate sector. Since their advent, both streams of public and private security have contributed complimentary, and, at times, convergent pieces of the broader liberal capitalist security regime that literally constitutes citizens in the image of pacified consumers - those who participate in orderly competitive market relations in such a fashion as to produce liberal capitalist notions of what security is, through the mechanisms that liberal capitalist security considers to be the appropriate avenues towards the achievement of that security: sometimes discipline (entailing surveillance and control of access to reward) and, where discipline fails, coercion.

The dichotomy that has been drawn between 'public policing' and 'private security' is largely illusory, but very deeply entrenched within our dominant conceptual frameworks for political economy. Undertaking a brief genealogy of the modern Western policing concept is highly illustrative in this regard, and thereby helps us to think beyond this false dichotomy.

Policing as pacification

It surprises many to know that the very word 'police' has its origins in the notion of 'policy'.[15] This is to say that in the sixteenth and seventeenth centuries in Europe, 'police' literally meant all activity undertaken by the government to ensure the integrity of the polity and what was defined by the governors as the 'well-being' (i.e., *bien être*) of the population.[16] As we have seen shifts in ways of thinking about society, the economy, and the polity, our definition of 'good policy' has changed, and with it our understanding of what 'police' is.

The rise of 'free' and growing markets through the seventeenth and eighteenth centuries produced the material wealth (i.e., capital) that literally funded the project of building a centrally-administered nation-state that *could* muster a range of large public agencies and services. Mercantilists, who sought to privatize the holdings of the feudal barons, thus considered in common with the king (who stood much to gain by weakening this same landed gentry) that the path to human well-being was through guaranteeing the conditions that would permit for continued market growth – beneficial to the merchants of course, and to their sovereign who would thereby have the resources and thus enhanced capacity to maintain the foundational order upon which markets could thrive. Thus, policing at this stage of mercantilist political economy entailed all manner of state-led initiatives in market space – such as setting import tariffs so as to strike the right balance between imports and exports – to secure corporate interests so as to ensure market health (defined as growth).

At the time that the science of economics - founded, as it was, upon advances in statistical methods - began to see and so think of markets as things possessed of their own internal logics and 'natural' processes best left alone to flourish, recipes and techniques for policing shifted profoundly, but the underlying purposes remained constant. Specifically, policing moved away from direct market intervention in the private sphere towards the enforcement of law and moralistic discipline in the public sphere – simply a different recipe for laying the foundational order upon which it was hoped that markets could flourish to generate the capital that would fund the mechanisms of social order. Within this novel liberal capitalist scheme of security, social order would be maintained not through underwriting a powerful and imposing sovereign, but rather through eliciting public cooperation through the offer of individual reward for engaging in 'appropriately' (but not excessive or violent) competitive liberal capitalist market relations.

At its heart, liberal capitalism believes that such competition between individuals will produce innovation and thus expanding markets and so sufficient wealth (essentially, that which has since been demonstrated to be just slightly beyond outright penury for the masses) to keep 'good citizens' passively engaged in the pursuit of their own little sliver of capital, and thus orderly. Such a political economy would require a policing system that would enforce the morals and docility of conscientious workers who would assume the roles of appropriately competitive and consumptive citizens. It would require a pacifying policing system premised upon corrective discipline (i.e., for those already civilized or at least sociable), and, where necessary, repressive sovereignty (i.e., for those considered to be so far beyond redemption as to be literally 'feckless' – incapable of assuming responsibility, and so being governed through, the civilizing process). Within the conceptual context of liberalism, therefore, *police* as a concept came to reflect the limited meaning of 'enforcing the law and upholding morals in public space' (at least in the ideal case). Over the late-eighteenth and into the nineteenth centuries, all other *policy* that was directed towards controlling the private (market and civil) realm came to be known as *regulation*.[17]

Henceforth, policing and regulation were not only conceptually separated at the level of abstract political economic philosophy, it followed that they were separated at the level of the law, institutional structures, practices, and thus organizational identities and images. Thus, Western society began to *imagine* that public security produced through the public police was something totally different and separate from the corporate security and private order delivered under non-state authority and through non-state actors. In reality, however, action in both the public and private realm was orientated towards the fundamental purpose of assuring the *growth of markets through which public benefit was thought to be/presented as being attainable.*[18] Private security and public policing thus share their origins in the same liberal capitalist set of beliefs concerning how best to achieve human well-being through apparently infinite market expansion.

Driving yet another stake into the argument that the state might be *assumed*, as a matter of theoretical or democratic principle, to act as the best guarantor of social safety, is the myth-status of the view that the locus or place of origin of uniformed, 'professional' policing was the public sphere. In fact, there was a great deal of opposition to the development of public policing institutions in Britain, not only amongst the poorer classes, but also within the political class, who were deeply suspicious of any centralized institutionalization of policing authority.[19]

It was only through a gradual public "familiarisation with extraordinary powers and institutional technologies" first developed in the private sphere, that moral entrepreneurs such as Patrick Colquhoun and Robert Peel were able to push forward their agendas for professionalized, salaried public policing. Significant in this regard were the mid-eighteenth century examples of the corporate-sponsored and -recruited Bow Street Runners in London, who were charged with the task of securing the transport of materials and goods back and forth from the ports of the Thames and factories of the city, along with corporate-led efforts to secure the rural, factory-centred 'company towns' of the mid-18th century.[20] And yet, even on the back of such public familiarisation with extraordinary corporate policing technologies, champions of public policing reform were only able to initiate these institutions on the sidelines of public vision in the first colony of Ireland by the turn of the 19th century: efforts to consolidate public policing 'at home' in the Metropole would not succeed until 1829, a point in time over a half-century *after* private security had led the charge to professionalized and remunerated security services. Private innovation, in other words, led public policymaking in the domain of modern policing,[21] and both sets of initiatives were intended to produce the type of order that was conducive to ensure the growth of markets.

Seen in these terms, it is a strange suggestion indeed to respond to the socially-corrosive effects of private security through the retrenchment of the opposite face of the same security coin, minted in the common image of pacification for capital growth and expansion. What then, are we to do about the problem? To begin to forge an answer to this set of questions, it is useful to begin with a survey of contemporary state-led efforts to 'democratically anchor' private security, as examples of what is inadequate to the task. The point can again be made that these efforts are inadequate in both practical and conceptual terms.

Public, private and the myth of 'democratizing security'

State government responses to the challenge of coordinating public-private security partnerships in pro-social directions have been very slow off the mark. As Shearing has elaborated, the state and its institutions have generally pursued a program of 'denial' with respect to the increasing authority and general capacity of what are, in effect, 'private governments' in contemporary advanced capitalism.[22] Thus, although the most active phase in the 'quiet revolution' in the contemporary resurgence of the private security industry began as early as the 1970s and accelerated over the course of the 1980s, governments have developed only the most limited forms of regulatory legislation throughout this period.[23] As the analysis above would suggest, this is perhaps unsurprising given the complimentary nature of public and private contributions to capitalist security.

At the level of practice, public police have been working with private security agencies for decades. Understandably, given their professional role, Police Federations have loudly resisted plans to develop any form of formalized partnership policing that appears to reduce the role of the public police in contemporary policing. As such, the majority of partnership policing that has developed has been until very recently *ad hoc* in nature, consisting mostly of informal information sharing between public and private policing agencies mixed with uneasy tensions at the borders and spill-over areas surrounding the corporatized new forms of communal space which continue to be the principal - but certainly by no means exclusive - domains of activity of the private security industry.[24]

Away from the media glare, and in the domain of legislative reform, public police agencies have responded to their own perceived deficiencies of these arrangements – and have drawn upon the repeated academic calls for government action to 'democratically anchor' the industry – to take the lead in pressuring government for the development of industry regulations. At the same time, private security agencies themselves have taken a lead role in developing their own 'industry standards', along with actively seeking to shape the governmental agenda for state regulation of the industry.

In many cases, corporate backing for governmental regulation of the private security industry can be understood as seeking the democratic imprimatur of satisfying (minimalistic) state standards - something which is much easier for large and well-capitalised corporate security firms to do than smaller outfits.[25] Such processes, however, will more than likely drive the industry towards the well-established structural capitalist tendency to consolidate corporate authority in ever larger conglomerate, multinational entities. The conglomeration of mega-security firms will likely contribute to the expansion of inappropriate security activity in the private security sector: by capitalism's own principles, a diminution in number of agencies that are in competition with one another will decrease the net amount of 'moral suasion' that exists in a network of service providers.[26] There will simply be fewer agencies in existence who have a material competitive incentive to call one another out on non-democratic or otherwise abusive activities: if a very small number of huge agencies are *all* engaged in abusive and other questionable practices, there will be no competitive advantage for seeking to be a lone ethical company; rather, advantage will accrue to all actors who cut corners in engaging questionable security practices in what essentially becomes a 'race to the bottom', covering what is in effect a very stable market-share between huge companies that have nowhere to grow.

On the back of these state and corporate 'pressures' to democratically anchor the private security industry, we have seen a number of legislative initiatives in Britain[27] continental Europe[28], Canada,[29] Australia, South Africa and elsewhere, which, despite their differences in detail, hold the common design objective of 'professionalizing' private security.

First, all of these legislative initiatives have developed industry standards to deal with licensing, attached to minimal standards for training and quality control of employees entering the industry. Second, there has been a consistent concern to address the symbols and appearance of private security agents, so as to ensure that they do not falsely represent a public security identity. Third, these legislative initiatives have sought to clarify questions concerning legitimate and illegitimate uses of coercion on the part of the industry - principally through underlining the particular legal rights to use force and in what instances as are specified in existing law, and also through the creation of new *codes of conduct* (which carry less authoritative force than formal pieces of legislation) which regulate the use of force in 'grey areas'. Fourth, and finally, there has been a concern to create avenues for public complaint against private security actors. Complaints can currently be made in most jurisdictions to specially-created public registrars in the pertinent government regulatory office, and/or directly to the public police themselves.

Overall, within such schemes, the state has been concerned to codify rules, and that the public police have been given a central role in enforcing such rules. In essence, therefore, efforts to 'democratically anchor' the private security industry have to date deployed classical command-and-control 'hierarchical' systems for regulation, wherein the state sets (through consultation) standards for the industry that are necessary to obtain operating licenses, and, where violated, will be policed through public agents and state-enforced penalty.

While such limited efforts to 'democratically anchor' private security may appear to hold some promise, it is equally if not more important not lose sight of the bigger picture of the underlying *purposes* of state and private capitalist security: state-driven professionalisation of the industry will be of little use towards human emancipation and planetary well-being, if professionalisation works towards rendering more efficient and effective capitalist security regimes that pacify citizens in the image of good producers and consumers. Indeed, as intimated above, state-driven professionalisation of the industry may serve to legitimise capitalist corporate security through awarding it the patina of democratic legitimacy.

Supporting the development of an alternative political imagination, then, must begin by challenging the dominant ideology which understands human security in terms of rule-enforcement and disciplinary surveillance in service of the expansion of markets. As the analysis indicates, we are not going develop such an imagination in the realm of either public or private security in their current guise; at issue is the discovery and experimentation with alternative approaches to human solidarity and well-being.

Notes

1. An argument aligned with that presented by Mark Neocleous, *Critique of Security*. (Montréal and Kingston: McGill-Queen's University Press, 2008).
2. See, for example, Clifford Shearing and Philip Stenning, 'Private Security: Implications for Social Control', *Social Problems*, Vol. 30, No. 5, 1983, pp. 493-506; Steven Spitzer and Andrew Scull, 'Privatization and Capitalist Development: The Case of the Private Police', *Social Problems*, Vol. 25, No. 1, 1977, pp. 18-29.
3. In overview, see, Les Johnston, *The Re-birth of Private Policing* (London: Routledge, 1992); Michael Kempa, Ryan Carrier, Jennifer Wood and Clifford Shearing, 'Reflections On the Evolving Concept of 'Private Policing', *European Journal on Criminal Policy and Research*, Vol. 7, No. 2, 1999, pp. 197-223.
4. See, for example, Johnston, *The Rebirth of Private Policing*; Shearing and Stenning, 'Private Security: Implications for Social Control'.
5. Philip Stenning, 'Powers and Accountability of the Private Police', *European Journal on Criminal Policy et Research*, Vol. 8, 2000, pp. 325-352; Neil Walker, *Policing in a Changing Constitutional Order* (London: Sweet and Maxwell, 2000).
6. Johnston, *Rebirth of Private Policing*; George Rigakos, *The New Para-Police: Risk Markets and Commodified Social Control* (Toronto: University of Toronto Press, 2002); Clive Williams, 'Constables for Hire: the History of Private "Public" Policing in the UK', *Policing and Society*, Vol. 18, No. 2, 2008, pp. 190-205.
7. Rigakos, *New Para-Police*; Anne-Marie Singh, 'Private Security and Crime Control', *Theoretical Criminology*, Vol. 9, No. 2, 2005, pp. 153-74; Stenning, 'Powers and Accountability of the Private Police'.
8. Michael Kempa, Philip Stenning, and Jennifer Wood, 'Policing Communal Spaces: A Reconfiguration of the 'Mass Private Property' Hypothesis', *British Journal of Criminology*, Vol. 44, No. 4, 2004, pp. 562-81; Darren Palmer and Chad Whelan, 'Policing in the "Communal Spaces" of Major Event Venues', *Police Practice and Research: An International Journal*, Vol. 8, No. 5, 2007, pp. 401-414; Alison Wakefield, *Selling Security: The Private Policing of Public Space* (Cullompton: Willan: 2003); Andrew Von Hirsch

and Clifford Shearing, 'Exclusion From Public Space', in Andrew Von Hirsch, David Garland, and Alison Wakefield (eds.), *Ethical and Social Perspectives on Situational Crime Prevention* (Oxford and Portland, Oregon: Hart Publishing).

9   Michael Kempa, 'Academic Engagement of International Policing Reform Assistance: Putting Foucauldian Genealogy to Practical Use', *The Canadian Journal of Criminology and Criminal Justice*, Vol. 52, No. 3, 2010, pp. 271-283.

10 See, for example, Shearing and Stenning, 'Private Security'.

11 In overview, see Shearing and Stenning, 'Private Security'; Michael Kempa and Anne-Marie Singh, 'Private Security, Political Economy and the Policing of Race: Probing Global Hypotheses Through the Case of South Africa', *Theoretical Criminology*, Vol. 12, No. 3, 2008, pp. 333-354; Rigakos, *New Para-Police*; Von Hirsch and Shearing, 'Exclusion From Public Space'.

12 Ian Loader and Neil Walker, *Civilizing Security* (Cambridge: Cambridge University Press, 2007); see also: Lucia Zedner, 'Liquid Security: Managing the Market for Crime Control', *Criminology and Criminal Justice*, Vol. 6, No. 3, 2006, pp. 267-288.

13 In overview, see, Robert Reiner, *The Politics of the Police*, 3rd edition, (Oxford: Oxford University, 2000); Wesley Pue, *Pepper in our Eyes: The APEC Affair* (Vancouver: UBC Press, 2000).

14 On the process of tinkering with a 'scientific model' for democratic police governance, see: Michael Kempa, 'Tracing the Diffusion of Policing Governance Models From the British Isles and Back Again: Some Directions for Democratic Reform in Troubled Times', *Police Practice and Research: An International Journal*, Vol. 8, No. 2, 2007, pp. 107 – 123.

15 Michel Foucault, *Security, Territory, Population* (New York: Palgrave Macmillan, 2007).

16 Foucault, *Security, Territory, Population*, Ch. 12.

17 Foucault, *Security, Territory, Population*; Peter Gill, 'Policing and Regulation: What Is the Difference?', *Social and Legal Studies*, Vol. 11, No. 4, 2002, pp. 523-546.

18 See especially Mark Neocleous, 'Policing and Pin Making: Adam Smith, Police and the State of Prosperity', *Policing and Society*, Vol. 8, 1998, pp. 425-449; Neocleous, *Critique of Security*, Ch. 4.

19 Reiner, *Politics of the Police*.

20 Spitzer and Scull, 'Privatization and Capitalist Development'.
21 See especially: Clive Williams, 'Constables for Hire: The History of Private "Public" Policing in the UK', *Policing and Society*, Vol. 18, No. 2, 2008, 190-205, see also Clifford Shearing 'The Unrecognized Origins of the New Policing: Linkages Between Public and Private Policing', in Mark Felson and Ronald Clarke (eds.), *Business and Crime Prevention* (Monsey, NY: Criminal Justice Press. 1997).
22 Clifford Shearing, 'Reflections On the Refusal to Acknowledge Private Governments', in Jennifer Wood and Benoit Dupont (eds.), *Democracy, Society and the Governance of Security* (Cambridge: Canbridge University Press, 2006).
23 See for example: Mark Button, 'Beyond the Public Gaze: The Exclusion of Private Investigators from the British Debate over Regulating Private Security', *International Journal of the Sociology of Law*, Vol. 26, No. 1, 1998, pp. 1-16; Mark Button, M. 'Assessing the Regulation of Private Security across Europe', *European Journal of Criminology*, Vol. 4, No. 1, 2007, pp. 109-28.
24 Mark Button, *Security Officers and Policing: Powers, Culture and Control in the Governance of Private Space* (Aldershot: Ashgate, 2007).
25 See Zedner, 'Liquid Security'.
26 Steve Tombs and David Whyte, 'Scrutinizing the Powerful: Crime, Contemporary Political Economy and Critical Social Research', in Steve Tombs and David Whyte (eds.), *Unmasking the Crimes of the Powerful* (New York: Peter Lang, 2003).
27 In Britain, see Button, *Security Officers and Policing*.
28 For a European overview, see: Button, 'Assessing the Regulation of Private Security across Europe'; Andrea Gimenez-Salinas, 'New Approaches Regarding Private/Public Security', *Policing & Society: An International Journal of Research & Policy*, Vol. 14, No. 2, 2004, pp. 158-74.
29 On Canada see Wendy Cukier, T. Quigley and J. Susla, J. 'Canadian Regulation of Private Security in an International Perspective', *International Journal of the Sociology of Law*, Vol. 31, No. 3, 2003, pp. 239-65.

[4]

War on the Poor: Urban Poverty, Target Policing and Social Control

GAETAN_HEROUX

The social chaos and violence that have entrenched themselves in Toronto's poor communities as a result of major cutbacks to social programs over the last three decades has led to an escalation of law-and-order policies and the need to control the social disorder in poor neighbourhoods. Since the early 1990s Toronto politicians have supported the implementation of numerous 'target policing' programs in poor communities, and in the city's commercial and financial districts, in an attempt to address the growing drug trade and violence which now dominate the lives of people in many of the city's poor neighbourhoods. Government officials fear this social unrest, but their refusal to provide the city's poorest citizens with safe affordable housing and sufficient income has led to the creation of new laws that criminalize the poor, the hiring of more police officers, the building of new prisons, and the demand for tougher jail sentences in an attempt to control the city's impoverished neighbourhoods. The primary function of the police in these poor communities is to control social unrest in the absence of social programs. The growing resources now being provided to the police to fight the War on Drugs in poor areas of the city are nothing less than a War on the Poor.

The Making of a Crisis

The 1980's and 1990's marked a fundamental change in government social policies in many countries around the globe. In England, in the 1980s, Margaret Thatcher's governments began the process of dismantling the country's welfare state. In the latter part if the 1990s Tony Blair's governments continued these attacks, with the Labour government responsible for making major cuts to the country's social programs. Across the Atlantic similar attacks against the United States social safety net were implemented by Ronald Regan in the 1980s. It was, however, the Clinton regime which enacted some of the most draconian cuts to welfare programs. Canada's social programs were also coming under attack during these two decades. Brian Mulroney's Progressive Conservative Party came to power in late summer of 1984. Soon after the Tories were elected they made cuts to the federal unemployment insurance program. By 1990 Mulroney's government had frozen transfer payments to three of Canada's largest provinces - British Columbia, Alberta, and Ontario. The provinces depended on this federal transfer payments to help cover welfare costs. In the fall of 1993 Jean Chretien's Liberal Party defeated the Conservatives. Chretien's social policies, however, moved even further to the right than that of the Tories. Chretien wasted no time in taking action and over the next two to three years his government was responsible for implementing some of the most drastic cuts to social programs that the country has ever seen. In 1993 the federal government eliminated the country's national housing program, and the following year Paul Martin, Minister of Finance, announced that the federal government would be slashing unemployment benefits by $5.5 billion dollars over a three-year period. "Major, major, cuts are going to affect every sector of our society", Martin warned the provinces. "We have told the provinces that they have two years in which to complete with us the end of this process. And that at the end of that two years we will be taking massive amounts of money out of the federal-provincial structure".[1] This transfer money was used by the provincial governments to help them cover the cost of social programs such as welfare, education, and health care. The cut to transfer payments caused many of the provinces to slash their welfare rates and to make major cuts to other social programs.

In the summer of 1995 Mike Harris's Conservatives came into power in the province of Ontario. One of Harris's key platforms was to slash welfare rates. In the early fall of 1995 the Tories cut welfare rates by 21.6 per cent in Ontario. New regulations were also introduced making it more difficult for people to access welfare in Ontario. In January 1996 the Harris government announced the cancellation of the construction of 17,000 units of social housing. Several years later the provincial Conservatives downloaded the responsibility for the maintenance of socialhousing to the municipal governments. Major reforms were also made to the Landlord and Tenant Act. The new act, now called the Tenant Protection Act, removed rent control on rental units that became vacant and made it easier for landlords to evict tenants. On January 31, 2000, the Safe Streets Act, which criminalized beggars and squeegeers, came into effect.

Harris's policies had an immediate impact on people living in Toronto's poor communities. East Downtown Toronto has one of the largest concentrations of social housing in Canada, including Regent Park. East Downtown Toronto is also home to Seaton house, Canada's largest men's hostel. A whole infrastructure has been established in the area over the last century to try and meet the needs of Toronto's homeless population. As a result of Harris's welfare cuts people on social assistance in East Downtown Toronto were unable to meet some of their most basic needs. Other poor neighbourhoods, such as Parkdale, in the west end of downtown Toronto, the Jamestown social housing project in Rexdale and the social housing project in Jane and Finch, which were located in the north end of the city, were also severely affected. These poor com-munities were subsequently identified has high crime risk and have been targeted with special policing programs since the early 1990's.

Federal and provincial cuts to social programs, implemented since the early 1980's, have been responsible for the huge explosion of homelessness that is now being experienced in every major urban centre across Canada. Nowhere has this crisis been felt more than in Toronto. Several weeks after Mike Harris cut welfare rates, Toronto's homeless shelters were over-flowing. A few weeks after these cuts were implemented Seaton House was forced to put mattresses in the hallways to deal with the increased demand for shelter by homeless men. Dennis Fotinos, head of the Human Services Committee, said that the demand for hostel beds that the city was experiencing was the greatest since the Great Depression.[2] When three homeless men froze to death in January 1996, the Canadian Army, at the request of the city, opened the Moss Park Armouries as an emergency homeless shelter for two weeks to help relieve the overcrowding in city shelters. By mid-summer of that year landlords in the city were filing 600 applications for evict tenants every week. This was a 40 per cent increase over applications made during the same period in 1995.

In early 1998, Mayor Mel Lastman appointed Ann Golden, president of the United Way, to head a task force to investigate the city's growing homelessness problem. In the fall of 1998 Toronto declared homelessness a national disaster and requested help from the federal government to address the homeless crisis. Golden's final report on the state of homelessness in Toronto was released in January of 1999. The task force found that youth and families with children accounted for the largest increase of people seeking shelter. Golden's investigation found that from September 1992 to September 1998 the number of youth using shelters had increased by 80 per cent, families by 123 per cent, and adults by 63 per cent. In the spring of 1999 Toronto held the first ever National Summit on Homelessness in an attempt to get the provincial and federal governments to take action around the homeless crisis.

Despite the findings of Ann Golden's Task Force on Homelessness and Mayor Mel Lastman's hosting of the National Summit on Homelessness in Toronto, the city failed to get the provincial and federal governments to commit any substantial amount of resources for housing and income support programs, which were essential in order to address the city's homeless crisis. As a result Toronto was unable to contain its homeless crisis. The Fort York Armouries, located the city's west-downtown, was used as an emergency homeless shelter throughout most of 1999. That summer John Jagt, head of Toronto's hostel services, was forced to open the doors of Metro Hall to the homeless. "This is a crisis", a frustrated Jagt told the press. "We've never been in this kind of position at the beginning of the summer. We're not on top of it, we're chasing it . . . I don't see a light at the end of the tunnel".[3] With winter coming, the city estimated that it needed another 700 shelter beds. What Jagt failed to point out was the politically constructed nature of the crisis, as we shall see.

Over the following 5 years the crisis got worse. On the one hand, by the summer of 1999 an estimated 1,000 homeless men and women were choosing to stay outdoors - in the city's downtown parks, along the Don Valley River, and under the Gardner Expressway - rather than risk entering the overcrowded and dangerous city shelters, many surviving by panhandling, squeegeeing and by using local drop-ins and eating at the various charitable soup kitchens. By the summer of 2002 there were more than 100 homeless men and women squatting a piece of polluted land by the lake shore, which was owned by Home Depot. Nathan Philip Square, located directly in front of city hall, was also used regularly by homeless people who were seeking refuge there during the night. By the fall of 2004 more than 100 homeless men and women were sleeping in front of City Hall on a nightly basis. On the other hand, the presence of thousands of homeless and destitute people begging and living in extreme poverty in the city's downtown core created extreme tension. Local business associations and residents associations complained that panhandlers and squeegee kids were hurting business, scaring away tourists, and affecting their quality of life. As the homeless crisis grew demands were made to clear and sweep the downtown core of these undesirables. Into this situation came new initiatives: Project 35, Project 40, Community Action Policing (CAP), and Toronto Anti-Violence Intervention Strategy (TAVIS). And with these initiatives, the politically constructed nature of the crisis becomes clear.

Choosing targets

Project 35 was first introduced into Toronto's poor communities in the fall of 1993. It was implemented in three poor communities that had been identified as having high crime areas. The small project targeted Parkdale, Bloor Street West to Landsdown, and Kensington Market, all located in west downtown Toronto. Drugs and prostitution were the main targets. Over a two month period that fall uniformed officers, working overtime, flooded the targeted areas in the late evenings. Officers worked closely with the business associations and local residents association to identify establishments that attracted drug and criminal activities. Deputy Chief Clark reported that officers involved this new initiative visited "liquor licence establishments, parks, businesses premises and community centres and enforced Federal, Provincial Municipal laws".[4]

Project 35 had three fundamental problems. The first problem was that officers working on the project were paid overtime and this was very expensive. Secondly, the new initiative only succeeded in moving the problem to other areas of the city. In his report to the Police Services Board Deputy Chief Clarke wrote that "it was anticipated at the commencement of the project that if extra police officers were deployed in the Bloor-Landsdown area of No. 14 Division, the problem would just move across into No.11 Division. By policing this area in joint operation, it addressed both Divisions at the same time and the problem moves, it will move out of the area".The most serious problem however was that the project was short term. Funding for Project 35 was limited. What would happen when the project ended? Deputy Chief Clark conceded that without maintaining a high police presence in the targeted areas the street level crime would return. "Without the additional financial human resources to maintain high levels of police enforcement", Deputy Chief Clarke told the members of the Police Services Board, "it is anticipated, unfortunately, that the targeted areas would with the coming of spring, start to increase in criminal activity".[5] Since the underlying causes of the poverty experienced by the poor living in these communities remained, and were never substantially addressed, Project 35 was, in effect, merely a mechanism of class control.

Despite these obvious problems, in the summer of 1994 Project 35 was implemented in eight high-crime-risk areas. Parkdale and Landsdowne were again targeted, but the Project also targeted social housing projects in the northeast and northwest suburbs of Toronto. The cost of the new expended target initiative was $500,000. The program was to last for two months in each of the targeted communities.

Originally, Regent Park in East Downtown Toronto was not included as part of Project 35. Butafter several shootings occurred there in the summer and after representatives from Regent Park asked the Police Services Board for more police presence Project 40 was created to target crime in Regent Park. That same summer local residents' associations, made up of some of the more affluent resident that had moved to East Downtown Toronto over the last few decades, also attended a Police Service Board meeting. They requested that the Dundas East corridor, running from Yonge to River Sts., be included as part of Project 40. Residents, who often referred to the Dundas East corridor as 'Crack Alley', told members of the board that their neighbourhood was under siege from 'crack dealers and hookers'. Police agreed to include the Dundas East corridor as part of the Project 40 initiative. The area encompassed by Project 40 now included numerous homeless services, including Seaton House, two large drop-ins for the homeless operating out of All Saints Church and a large weekend drop-in located at Central Neighbourhood House. Homeless men and women who used these social programs were regularly targeted by Project 40.

Although the main focus of Project 35 and Project 40 was purportedly drugs and prostitution, people committing minor infractions and people involved in 'anti-social behaviour' also became prime targets. Words like 'zero tolerance' and 'quality of life' were now commonly used to describe target policing. "We are responding to a request of the community," Sgt. Doug Simms told the *Star*. "The project is zero tolerance . . .anything that goes down is taken down and drugs are the No. 1 concern".[6] Project 40 began on August 1, 1994, and ended on October 1. During this period police flooded the area in the evenings. *The*

Toronto Star described the new police anti-crime initiative as follows:

> 50 extra officers are joining 24 hour patrol by Church, Shuter, Gerrard, and River Street in what is known as Project 40...Mounted police, motorcycle patrols, emergency task force, tracking dog teams are joined by doubled-up foot patrols in the neighbourhood blitz.[7]

Intimidation and harassment of the homeless and of Regent Park residents occurred on a regular basis during the two-month blitz. This created an organized war of attrition between the police and the poor. On the evening of August 26, 1994, five days before Project 40 ended, tensions came to a head when Toronto police raided Allan Gardens, which was located outside the targeted area. The raid was Project 40's largest operation. More than 60 black men, some of whom had just finished playing a pick up soccer game, were rounded up by the police while members of the homeowners association – mainly white middle calls residents – cheered and clapped. The black men were made to sit on the ground with their hands on their heads. One by one they were asked for identification, searched, and questioned. Police entered their names in the computer looking for outstanding warrants and prior arrests. Half a dozen people were charged with criminal charges that evening; only two of these charges were drug related. In contrast, thirty five of the men were given $75 loitering tickets – that classic mechanism of police power – and this included some of those in the park playing soccer; as with most loitering charges the men were warned that they would be arrested if they returned to the park.

Following condemnation by members of the black community and local agencies who worked with the poor in the area, Chief McCormack argued that Toronto police were simply reacting to complaints by local residents associations when police made the decision to raid the Allan Gardens. "As a result of Project No. 35 and Project No.40", Chief William McCormick wrote, "the problem simply moved into another location – Allan Gardens".[8] Demonstrations were held to denounce the raid and deputations were later made to the Police Services Board. One of the agencies that was very critical of the raid was Central Neighbourhood House. Several of the soccer players rounded up in Allan Gardens belonged to the CNH indoor soccer team. Maureen Ford, president of CNH, made the following comments at the Police Services Board meeting on December 14, 1994:

> We believe that events of August 26 did not serve to create a safer community but was in fact damaging to the community relations, particularly with the Black community. We know that the police actions that night effectively served to ban a number of Black community members from using a public park, and taking part in lawful activities in Allan Gardens. We are deeply saddened and frustrated by the refusal of the police to apologize for the way in which many Black community members were treated that night. Most upsetting is the attitude I encountered throughout our meetings and in

the letter from Chief McCormack to Susan Eng on this issue, that everyone retained that night were somehow deserving of this treatment, despite that few were charges.⁹

Another agency, Parents for Better Beginnings, whose clients were residents of Regent Park, was also critical of the police's actions during the Allan Garden's raid. A letter written to Susan Eng, the chair of the Police Services Board, was very critical of the use of target policing and the targeting of black youth:

> Target policing and drug sweeps does nothing to prevent problems from re-surfacing. Police either have a low profile or they come in full force and exhibit an excessive use of power. This is not community policing, it is not responsible policing, and it clearly targets particular groups, of which the police had ongoing struggles . . . many residents see the police in riot gear tearing into their community and using excessive use of power to arrest and round up alleged drug offenders, usually Black youth. This feeds into racism, classicism, tension, and a great fear by the community of the police and of the youth.¹⁰

The use of target policing in East Downtown Toronto failed to make the community safe and it did great damage to community relations. A year later tensions between black residents living in Regent Park and the police exploded. When police attempted to arrest a black man outside the community centre more than 100 Regent Park residents confronted police officers and a riot ensued. Forty-five police cruisers responded to the and eight officers were injured during the confrontation.

Very few people believed that target policing programs like Project 35/40 would do anything to stop the violence or address the safety issues raised by people living in poor communities. Linda Hurst, a *Toronto Star* reporter, was very sceptical about the police force's ability to make poor communities safer through such programs.

> Okay, so nobody thinks it will work long term. Not the residents, not the police, and assuredly not the dealers. No way the current two month blitz is going to permanently rid Regent Park and surrounding street of drug related crime. Come October, they'll come back.[11]

Doubts were also expressed by Father Day, a Catholic Priest in Regent Park, who was one of the deputants who had asked the Police Services Board for help after the shootings in Regent Park: "It [target policing] didn't cut one iota on drugs. Every arrest creates a job opening, dealer, courier, whatever, and there are thousands of unemployed people here just waiting to be hired". Four months after Project 35 and Project 40 ended some officers from 51 Division were also acknowledging that target policing was having very little effect in addressing social concerns of the residents living in East Downtown Toronto. "Police admit", Howard Mascol, a *Star* reporter, wrote, "that after decades of hard-line policing, the area is still rife with firearms, drugs, poverty-induced racial problems, public drunkenness and homelessness".[12] Despite these criticisms and recognition that target policing had failed the Toronto police force continued to implement target policing projects in poor communities across the city. Here as elsewhere, the War on the Poor would be permanent one.

War on Squeegees

By the time Community Action Policing (CAP) was introduced in the summer of 1999, the city of Toronto had unofficially embraced the 'broken window' theory. Proponents of this theory argued that cracking down on 'petty crimes' and 'anti-social behaviour,' such as panhandling and squeegeeing, would result in a decrease in major crimes. The year before Community Action Policing was implemented Premier Mike Harris and Mayor Mel Lastman declared war on squeegee kids and on panhandlers. Harris and his government played an instrumental role in the summer of 1998 in feeding the Squeegee Wars. In February 1998, Toronto hosted a two-day international conference on crime control. The conference was organized by the Ontario Crime Control Commission, which consisted of three Tory back benchers. The chair of the commission was Conservative MPP Jim Brown. The key speaker at the conference was George Kelling, the criminologist responsible for developing the 'broken window' theory. The *Toronto Star* reported that Kelling told the audience that "the key to reversing crime rates is to crack down on the most visible kinds of social disorder, such as aggressive beggars even squeegee kids".[13] There were no laws in Toronto against squeegeeing and panhandling at the time. Nevertheless, this did not prevent the police from trying to run squeegeers and panhandlers out of the downtown core. To do this they used a gamut of discretionary police powers, giving out tickets to squeegeers and panhandlers for such things as impeding traffic, jaywalking, operating a bike without a bell, dwelling in a park without a permit, blocking a sidewalk, trespassing and littering. "We're being directed to take action", Staff Sergeant Ken Kinsley told the Star. "My direction to my officers is that we don't drive by or go by a problem. And if we talk to people in the community, we're being directed very forcefully to take action against these people".[14]

Attempts by city Councillor Ila Bossoms to introduce a new city bylaw in June, which would have banned squeegeeing and fined panhandlers for asking for change "within ten meters of a transit stop, subway entrances, bank or automatic machines...[or] sit or lie on the sidewalk while asking for change or beg between sunset and sunrise," were rejected by the city's emergency and protective services committee. According to assistant city solicitor, Albert Cohen, the bylaw was unenforceable and would probably be subject to challenges under the Charter of Rights.

Nonetheless, the war had to be fought, and so after Bossoms' proposed bylaw was dismissed Mayor Mel Lastman described squeegee kids as 'thugs', 'pests, and 'lazy', promising to 'wipe them out' and 'run them out of town'. 'Mayor: It's War On Squeegees', ran the front page of the *Toronto Sun* on 23 July. Several days earlier Premier Mike Harris directed Commissioner

Jim Brown to find a solution to the squeegee and panhandling problem. Commissioner Brown warned that Toronto would become the 'squeegee capital of the world' if they didn't act. "Something needs to be done", Brown told the *Toronto Star*. "We'd like to see Toronto cleaned up".[15] That summer Toronto saw massive police sweeps targeting squeegee kids and pan-handlers. One week in mid-July, police sweeps led to the arrests of more than 30 squeegee kids. The Tory's crime commission set up a phone hot line whereby Ontarians could express their views on how to deal with squeegeers and panhandlers. In the spring of 1999 Mike Harris's Tories released their election platform. Harris promised to crackdown on 'welfare cheats', 'squeegee kids' and 'aggressive panhandlers'. On June 10, 1999, the Tories were re-elected and squeegee kids and panhandlers became public enemy number 1 once again, but in the eyes of the political Right behind the squeegee kid and aggressive panhandler stood that classic enemy in the War: the welfare cheat.

In July Toronto announced that it was implementing its new Community Action Policing initiative. Nineteen 'hot spots', which the police refused to identify, were to be targeted, with squeegee kids and panhandlers being the main targets. According to Chief David Boothby, drugs and prostitutions were not his only concerns: "We'll be cracking (down) on prostitutes, squeegee kids, vandals, drugs – things that are very obvious and annoying to the public at large".[16] The new $1.9 million initiative began on July 15, ran for 11 weeks and employed 175 uniform officers, who were again paid overtime. Despite the absence of any new bylaw police intimidation and harassment of the poor during the CAP program was rampant. There were numerous reports by social workers, the poor and the homeless of harassment and intimidation. Those targeted complained of being constantly searched, questioned, photographed, ticketed and told that they had to move on. It was common for the police to push squeegeers and panhandlers out of their division where the officers no longer had to deal with them and where squeegers and panhandlers would become the problem of officers in other divisions. The following is just one example of an encounter between a police officer and two squeegee kids, which appeared in the Toronto Star. The two youth were targeted at the corner of Spadina Ave. and Queen St., a well known spot where squeegee youth hung out:

> Riga and her friend Francis Dugal were approached by Constable Everett Elliott. Elliott spotted Dugal squeegeeing a car without a driver's permission, a mischief offence. Dugal had already been charged once last week for mischief. "We're investigating them (squeegee kids) as often as we can, sometimes three or four times a day", Elliott said. He takes a Polaroid photograph of Dugal, even though he is not being charged. He jots down a description of both Dugal and Riga, asking her if her tattoo, a snake curling below the collar bone, is new. Next, Elliott asks them where they're from, if they have any identification and notes the design of all their tattoos, the shade of their dreadlocks and the location of various

body piercings. This time, they're let off with a warning: "Squeegeeing isn't against the law yet, but it will be soon", Elliott says.[17]

In another account documented by Tom Lyons, a writer for Eye, a similar pattern emerges. Here the squeegee kids are threatened with arrest if they don't leave:

> It's July in Toronto, and the annual clash between cops and squeegee kids is unfolding as scheduled. At the corner of Queen and Spadina, three French-Canadian squeegee punks watch and mutter to each other as two officers approach. One of the cops shouts at them: "Fuck off? Why don't you go back to your own country?" - "I'm getting tired of this shit," says the other. After police take down descriptions of them on a notepad, one of the kids asks, "Is there anywhere we can go?" – "Anywhere that's not in my area," says the cop. "This is my corner now. The next time we find you here, we're going to charge you with trespassing and you'll spend the night in jail before seeing a judge in the morning."[18]

The information taken by officers, and recorded on contact sheets during these interrogations, is later entered into a police database. During the first week of CAP, officers completed 2000 contact sheets. By the end of the eleven week project, Toronto police boasted that they had made 955 arrests and that "officers contacted and/or investigated 62,282 people".[19]

Although no statistics are given regarding the number of tickets handed out during the CAP initiative, it is clear that the vast majority of people interrogated and investigated were not involved in any criminal activity.

On November 2, 1999, not long after the CAP project ended, Ontario's attorney general. Jim Flaherty, held a press conference in East Downtown Toronto. He released details of the proposed Safe Streets Act, whose main targets would be squeeggers and panhandlers. The new legislation proposed by the Tories would allow for fines ranging from $500 for a first offence and $1000 and/or jail for a second conviction. "Aggressive panhandling has to do with public safety", Flaherty claimed. "People have a right to walk on the sidewalk and drive on the street without being hassled, without being intimidated".[20]

The Safe Streets Act came into effect on January 31, 2000, as part of a renewal and expansion of Toronto's Community Action Policing initiative. Now costing $2.8 million the project, which began on June 10, 2000, would operate for sixteen weeks. This time, however, the police were armed with the Safe Streets Act. Police now had the tools to officially enforce the 'broken window' theory, even though 'zero tolerance' and the crackdown on 'anti-social behaviour' had unofficially been enforced by the police.

Surgical Strikes

In January 20006, the provincial liberal government announced a new $51 million program to fight crime. The announcement came after the high profile murder of a young woman who was shot while shopping with her family on Boxing Day in downtown Toronto. The money from the provincial government would be used to hire more police officers, 31 crown attorneys, and 3 new judges to deal with the growing violence in poor communities. The money would also be used to create a new target policing initiative – Toronto Anti-Violence Intervention Strategy (TAVIS).

Police officers working on the TAVIS project had identified 140 neighbourhoods in the city that needed attention, with 20 to 30 of these areas named as being high-risk. The project, which included three quick response teams of 18 cops each, two vans, and ten scout cars, was set up to gather intelligence and to target street level crime such as drugs, prostitutes and gangs. The Toronto police force presented the goal of TAVIS as wanting to create ties with the community and make people feel safe. "The police will blanket a neighbourhood with officers", Insp. Tom Fitzgerald said, "and . . .offer reassurance to communities that police are there to help".[21] Police representatives also described the new initiative as an 'in your face' program. "We're not putting up with this violence anymore", one officer told the *Toronto Star*.

Both Parkdale and East Downtown Toronto were again targeted and identified as high risk communities. Several social housing projects in the north end of the city would also receive special attention, as the poor were once again targeted, intimidated and harassed. Timothy Appleby, a Globe and Mail reporter, accompanied officers from TAVIS one evening. His observations provide some insight of how TAVIS waged war on the poor. The evening begins with a young black man in Parkdale, an alleged drug user, being swarmed, questioned, and eventually sent on his way by TAVIS officers. This scenario is repeated several times and by the end of the night Appleby questions this show of force, which seems to target the city's most vulnerable people:

> TAVIS officers, all in uniform, make their rounds of bars, strip joints, and coffee shops introducing themselves...and filling contact forms...this latest crime initiative deploys 18-officers teams who move around the city in small groups blanketing the 20 plus most high risk neighbourhoods for about a week at a time...As police made their rounds on Friday, it looked at times like overkill...At midnight the battered Waverly Hotel on Spadina looked similarly with firepower, as two impoverished transients were questioned and released.[22]

In the early morning hours of May 16, 2006, four-and-half months after TAVIS was introduced into poor neighbourhoods, 600 officers, using rams and stun grenades targeted the Jamestown social housing project in the north end of the city. The raid, the largest in the history of the Toronto police force, involved as many as seven different police forces, some coming from as far away as Montreal. The target, according to Chief Bill Blair, was the Jamestown Crew, who Blair argued had "the reputation of being the most violent gang city wide". By the end of the raid 100 arrests were made and more than 1000 criminal charges were laid. Many of those arrested and charged were young black men. "The leadership of the Jamestown Crew has been 'surgically' removed from the community", and the raid was carried out with "military precision", Blair informed the media at a press conference held later that day.[23]

Mayor David Miller was also quick to praise the raid, thereby reinforcing the view that law enforcement and incarceration continued to be the city's primary policy when it came to gangs and drugs, and the violence that had entrenched itself in some of Toronto's poorest neigh-bourhoods. "It's a very important sign to the people of Toronto and the people who have been living in neighbourhoods plague by violence", Miller said. "that where there are violent criminals, they will be apprehended and they will be put in jail".[24]

Residents of Jamestown who witnessed the pre-dawn raid felt differently and described the community as looking like 'a war zone'. Many residents were terrorized by the tactics used by the police that day. "You can't stick a gun at a . . .five-year-old kid, come on", Romona Gentles, a resident, argued. "Put yourself in my position. What if it was your daughter?". Other residents complained that police had busted down the wrong doors. "If you're going to investigate a person, make sure you know it's the right person you are getting," said Rouven Wilson, who was targeted, arrested and later released. "Don't go and kick down people's doors and try to hurt innocent people". Residents also reported that the door of a 76 year old grandmother was kicked in when police busted into her home looking for her grandson who was no there at the time.[25]

The following day residents were demanding to know where the programs were for the youth. "When are we going to see a bigger community centre in the Jamestown community?", asked Prince Gbekley. "You see (kids) in the street, they have nowhere to go. All they have to do is join gangs". Other residents described "how their kids needed homework clubs, after school programs, and basketball clubs".[26] There were no politicians there after the raid to announce any new major funding for jobs and social programs for youth. Many of the residents asked themselves the same question: Who will help them deal with the aftermath of the raid? Where was the support for the children and families that remained? The support would not come from their landlord, Toronto Community Housing, which is responsible for the management and maintenance of the city's social housing.

Soon after the raid Toronto Community Housing began implementing the process for mass evictions against families who had children arrested during the raid. Many of the families affected were single mothers who had other children that were not involved in any criminal activity. "Our concern is 'What is the activity that's taking place on property, what's the impact on the greater community?'"Steve Floros, the corporation's director of property, told the Toronto Star. "And our remedy, like any other landlord, is to turn to the tribunal and say "This is the issue, this is the tenant's involvement, and we're seeking a remedy, which is eviction in some cases"".[27]

Other social housing projects across the city were subsequently raided. TAVIS has now become a permanent fixture and it continues to be used against residents of poor neighbourhoods throughout the city, and in the city's downtown commercial and business districts. In 2007, Toronto police issued 10,584 Safe Streets Act tickets compared to 2,725 in 2004 – a 288 per cent increase.[28] In 2008 TAVIS arrested 2,640 people. Community contacts, or investigations and questioning of individuals by TAVIS that year was a record 109,796 people.[29]

Conclusion

TAVIS was introduced into poor neighbourhoods almost thirteen years after Project 35 was first implemented in west-downtown Toronto. The number of high-risk communities targeted grew from three to thirty, and the cost of operating TAVIS was ten times that of Project 35 and Project 40. The introduction and growth of such target policing initiaitives coincided with some of the largest cuts to social programs that the country had ever seen. Together, they have come to form a permanent War on the Poor. It is quite clear that the programs used to control social disorder in poor communities during a period of neo-liberal ascendancy. As the underlying causes of the poverty and violence that plague poor communities remains – indeed, are exacerbated by the policies in question - all three levels of governments are warning of further cuts to social programs. While the country still lacks a national housing program and welfare rates continue to be insufficient, the Safe Streets Act is used regularly against beggars and squeegeers by Toronto police.

This fundamental tension came to a head in the summer of 2010, when Toronto hosted the G20, an opportunity for the City to spend close to $1 billion dollars on 'security' to protect world leaders attending the summit. The combination of security measures and the arrest of more than 1,100 people (making it the largest mass arrest in the history of Canada) means that the period can only be understood in terms of that classic exercise in military-police power: martial law. "For the citizens of Toronto, the days up to and including the G20, will live in infamy as time and period of martial law set in the city", Andre Marin, Ontario's ombudsman warned.[30] Tactics used in target policing of poor neighbourhoods, such as stop-and-search and arbitrary arrests, were used throughout the G20 summit against protesters and Toronto citizens. In this context, the Generals leading the War on the Poor committed to implement austerity measures and to cut their country's massive deficits caused by the economic crisis over the last two years. The G20 epitomises the global civil war, of which Toronto's targeted policing initiatives are but one small part. Law and order policies combined with cuts in social programs: security and capital go hand-in-hand.

Notes

1. 'Worst Cuts Yet to come Martin Says', *The Toronto Star*, April 19, 1994.
2. '919 beds to be added for Metro homeless', *The Toronto Star*, October 27, 1995.
3. 'City turns Metro Hall into emergency shelter', *The Toronto Star*, June 5, 1999, and 'The bureaucrat who led the homeless to Metro Hall', *The Toronto Star*, June 8, 1999,
4. Extract from the Minutes of the Meeting of the Metropolitan Toronto Police Services Board held on March 03, 1994, #135 Pilot Project 35
5. #135 Pilot Project 35.
6. 'Regent Park welcomes police blitz', *The Toronto Star*, August 8, 1994.
7. "Police blitz gives project respite from pushers", *The Toronto Star*, August 8, 1994.
8. Wm. J. McCormack, Chief of Police *Metropolitan Toronto Police: Report on Allan Gardens*, December 6, 1994, p. 2.
9. Central Neighbourhood House Deputation, by Maureen Ford, President of Central Neighbourhood House, December 15, 1994
10. Letter to Ms. Susan Eng, Chairperson, Metro Toronto Police Services Board, fro, Parents for Better Beginnings, Correen Gilligan, Project Manager, December 09, 1994.
11. 'Police blitz gives project respite from pushers'.
12. 'Inside 51 Division: Metro's 'Fort Apache', *The Toronto Star*, February 4, 1995.
13. 'Petty crime crackdown saves cities: U.S. expert', *The Toronto Star*, February 13,1998.
14. 'Squeegee kids get squeezed', *The Toronto Star*, May 31, 1998.
15. ' "Nothing but thugs": Premier declares war in squeegee kids", *The Toronto Star*, July 22, 1998.
16. "Police target 'hot spots' in crackdown on city crime", *The Toronto Star*, July 6, 1999.
17. 'The crackdown: Police target squeegee kids', *The Toronto Star*, July 22, 1999; Tom Lyons, 'No money, no home, no rights: The police crackdown on street people and squeegee kids is popular, but it's illegal', August 5, 1999, EYE
18. Lyons, 'No money, no home, no rights'.
19. Toronto Police: 1999 Annual Report.

20 'New law targets squeegee kids, begging', November 3, 1999, The Toronto Star
21 '54 Police on hand to respond quickly', *The Toronto Star*, February 8, 2006.
22 'New police strategy designed to blanket high violence areas', *The Globe and Mail*, February 13, 2006.
23 'Gang leaders 'surgically removed' in 60 police raids', May 18, 2996, CBC Website.
24 'Showdown in Jamestown', *The Toronto Sun*, May 19, 2006,.
25 'Police raid in T.O ends in 78 arrests', May 18, 2006, Canadian Press, Global National Web site
26 'Police raids not enough, Jamestown residents say', CBC News, May 24, 2006.
27 'Family with gang "link" face eviction', *The Toronto Star*, January 24, 2007.
28 Ontario Coalition Against Poverty, *They Call It A Struggle For A Reason*, June 2008.
29 Toronto Police 2008 Annual Report.
30 'G20 regulations "likely illegal", Blasts Ontario Ombudsman', *The National Post*, December 8, 2010.

[5]
Poor Rogues and Social Police:
Subsistence Wages, Payday Lending and the Politics of Security

OLENA_KOBZAR

> Poor rogues, and usurers' men!
> Bawds between gold and want!
> William Shakespeare, *Timons of Athens*

Both classical economists of the nineteenth century and their most trenchant critic, Karl Marx, were in broad agreement about the economic vicissitudes which the working class faced in a competitive wage economy. Starting with the premise that there is a natural wage rate governed by the costs associated with reproducing labour power, these classical economists and their critical interlocutor understood that capitalism set in motion processes inclining market wages in the direction of a natural or subsistence level. But how that subsistence level should be conceived, and how implacable were the market processes disposing wages to approach that level, were questions that invited disagreement. For instance, while the preternaturally glum Malthus forecast an absolutely impoverished world of workers willfully reproducing themselves at a rate far in excess of that by which material productivity expanded, Ricardo, in his more optimistic moments, allowed that not only was the so-called 'natural wage' in part determined by those cultural and historical contingencies which established the norms of subsistence, but also that in certain circumstances continual investments in productivity might make possible a gradual increase in market wage rates. For his part, Marx more or less accepted the Ricardian view of natural and market wage rates, but saw the relationship of these two concepts as one fraught with contradictions. The contradictions arose, according to Marx, either because the inherent tendency of capitalism towards greater efficiencies meant the creation of an ever larger reserve army of labour whose presence would undermine market wage rates, or because even if, on the Ricardian supposition, market wage rates rose above a natural subsistence rate, the overall conditions of life for workers in a capitalist economy would still become commensurately more miserable as their control over the means of production vanished completely.

What was seen to be a vital debate in political economy in the nineteenth century increasingly gave way to dismissive platitudes in the latter half of the twentieth as the growth of a relatively affluent working class in developed capitalist economies seemed to have dispatched to the dustbin of intellectual history the concepts of an iron law of wages and the immiseration of the working class. The terms of art, 'fordism' and 'the Keyesian compromise', have been frequently used to explain in an abbreviated way the forces at work which produced this prosperous working class. According to these accounts, the deliberate pursuit of a high wage, mass consumption economy combined with a strategic political compromise between capital and labour combined to ensure workers would benefit from the wealth accumulation made possible by a rapidly expanding industrial capitalism. The latter compromise figures importantly in this standard explanation of relative labour affluence because it outlines the institutional mechanisms supposedly instrumental in its realization: a robust labour relations regime protective of union bargaining power; a supplementary social wage in the form of welfare benefits; and a macroeconomic policy-making system geared to maintaining full employment through demand management.

It is now nearly half a century since the height of the so-called 'golden age of capitalism' said to have been prompted by this coincidence of fordism and the Keynesian compromise. The intervening years have witnessed systematic economic restructuring at the firm, sectoral and national levels, a concomitant global reconfiguration of manufacturing, an unleashing of finance capital, a significant depreciation of the social wage, and an abandonment of classic demand management in favour of supply-side macroeconomic policies. Among the striking consequences of this neo-liberal turn, particularly in the last decade, has been the conspicuous widening of income disparities in those very developed economies that hitherto had boasted of having made obsolete old class distinctions.[1] Not only has the new millennium ushered in greater income inequalities in mature capitalist economies, especially evident in the Anglo-American nations of the U.K., U.S and Canada, but it has seen absolute increases in poverty levels. Associated with this latter trend has been the re-emergence of economic forms and practices that once had been intimately linked to the nineteenth century world of subsistence wages - things like pawnshops, wage assignments, installment purchasing, and payday lending.

In this chapter I examine the recent explosion of payday lending in the U.S., U.K. and Canada, in many ways the most vivid urban symbol of the new bifurcated economy that has become the legacy of neo-liberalism. I will argue that the phenomena of payday lending, and various recent state measures introduced to regulate this financial practice, illustrate just how a new security discourse has insinuated itself in contemporary social policy deliberations, a disciplining discourse that both recalls nineteenth century sentiments about the working poor and presages a future world of permanent underemployment for a plurality of workers. To grasp the significance of this new discourse of security, which I contend is a third historical variant of liberal governance, it pays to recollect the manner in which the working class was initially constituted as an object of administration at a time when industrial capitalism was becoming a hegemonic economic form and liberalism its political expression.

Contrary to its foundational myth in which an ascendant self-regulating private sphere was said to have established its relative autonomy from a circumscribed public sphere, the actual historical formation of liberal modes of governance depended crucially on the capacity of the state to promote particular forms of life conducive to the functioning and reproduction of a market economy. Central to this state project in the nineteenth century, as many have pointed out, were various measures supporting the commodification of labour.[2] Such measures included, in the seminal case of Britain, the Poor Law Amendment Act of 1834 calculated to help inculcate the routine of wage labour among the able-bodied poor, as well as a host of specific reform movements including health and hygiene campaigns intended to institute a quantum of order in the rapidly urbanizing centres of industrial capitalism. As Neocleous puts it, these several innovations can be usefully conceptualized by the term social policing, a term meant to signify a continuum in the practice of policing that includes both crime prevention and the social service work, all performed for the broader purpose of the maintenance of an emergent capitalist social order.[3]

One of the virtues of looking at such an ensemble of government practices as a project aimed at maintaining a social order defined by the needs of capitalism is that it allows one to see continuities between nineteenth century administrative policies towards the working poor and later twentieth century welfare policies ostensibly meant to elevate that same class. Thus rather that uncritically accept the customary depiction of welfare state capitalism as a major departure from an earlier laissez-faire capitalism, there are good reasons to think that former acted more to institutionalize and extend forms of social control that began with nineteenth century social policy aimed at creating a compliant and disciplined working class.[4] One very important way in which social control is exerted in this liberal form of governance is through what Burchell calls 'self-responsibilization' where efforts are made to integrate individuals into practices that work to govern them.[5] In the latter nineteenth and early twentieth centuries an array of charitable organizations, self-help societies, religious reform movements, and government agencies contributed to this technique of governance by encouraging the working poor to embrace habits of thrift, hygiene, sound domestic economy, familial responsibility, etc. The history of payday lending during this period illustrates this governance technique quite vividly.

The business of lending to the working poor, often intertwined with other commercial activities directed at this same class, became relatively common in the late nineteenth century in both the U.S. and Britain. In the U.S., for example, a widespread practice developed during the Civil War of merchants called 'sutlers' following Union army regiments as they moved from battlefield to battlefield, offering to advance funds or necessities to ill-provided soldiers in exchange for claims on their wages.[6] Roughly at the same time there arose in major cities in the eastern United States a category of lender called 'salary lenders' who typically sought out the relatively more secure workers in large industries and government institutions as customers for high-interest short-term loans at rates often in excess of 500% per annum.[7] Similar predatory lending practices materialized in Britain as tallymen and check traders transformed themselves into money lenders for the working poor by the late nineteenth century.[8] And throughout the period in both countries a host of related enterprises such as pawnshops and hire purchase schemes proliferated with the same purpose of supplying high interest loans to those who had no alternative sources of credit.

Unscrupulous as this class of credit providers may have been, civic reform responses to their perceived depredations are telling reminders that the modern liberal governance project had a particular type of moral and social regulation as its goal. The contours of that goal can be glimpsed from the activities of one of the key philanthropic agents in the U.S. promoting the cause of small loan reform: the Russell Sage Foundation. Created in 1907 by the widow of Russell Sage, a wealthy New York financier who controlled, among other assets, the fabled Western Union Company, the foundation almost from its inception focused its efforts on finding solutions to the problem of credit for the working poor by helping sponsor the creation of low-cost loan funds capitalized by philanthropically-minded financiers, and by advocating for legislative curbs on what were conventionally seen as usurious money lenders. The foundation had some success with the latter when different iterations of a model piece of legislation it had crafted in 1916, the Uniform Small Loans Law, were adopted by most state legislatures during the interwar years. In broad outline, the Uniform Small Loans Law aimed at controlling usurious lending by regulating small loan providers through a combination of licensing and disclosure requirements while at the same time authorizing such providers to charge interest at rates higher than those allowed for commercial banks so that they might realize reasonable profits on their outlays of capital. As a perceptive contemporary commentator pointed out at the time, one of the effects of the Uniform Small Loans Act, aside from affording borrowers a more transparent and capped rate structure for small loans, was to help provide a stable state-sanctioned regulatory environment for small loan providers, thus helping both to legitimate their enterprise and ensure their profit levels.[9]

Not only were the Small Loans Acts (and the variations on them which early twentieth century British and Canadian governments introduced in the form of Moneylenders Acts) a benefit to mainstream lenders who wished to penetrate the working-class credit market, but their underlying rationale was consistent with the self-responsibilization assignment envisaged by liberal governance. For intrinsic to these efforts to normalize credit facilities for the working poor was the objective of instilling in them habits of thrift, financial prudence and self-reliance, an aspiration succinctly affirmed by Mary Ellen Richmond, director of the charity department of the Russell Sage Foundation and a founder of modern American professional social work, when she related what she regarded as a well-known truism:

> The second class [of workers] includes those who are willing to work when work is plentiful, but who have little persistence or resourcefulness in procuring work. In the busy season they spend lavishly on cheap pleasures and soon become applicants for relief in troubled times….It is with the second class that the charitable may work lasting harm or lasting good. To let them feel that no responsibility rests with them during the busy season, and that all the responsibility rests with us to relieve their needs when the busy season is over, rapidly pushes them into [pauperism]. To teach them, on the other hand, the power and cumulative value of the saving habit, and so get them beforehand with the world, is to place them in the first class and soon render them independent of our material help.[10]

While the efforts of social formers eventually succeeded in curtailing much of the barely licit trade in predatory lending to the poor by the mid-twentieth century, it is useful to see this development as occupying a link between two variants of the overall project of the social policing of the working class. The first variant, as intimated in the views of social workers like Mary Richmond, was shaped by the need to create among workers a sense of self-responsibility that extended to matters of consumption and savings. This required the nurturing of habits of deferred gratification in the interests of general family financial prudence, behaviour that would relive charities and state agencies from the burden of maintaining workers during periods of unemployment, and just as significantly, would help ensure the reproduction of fit labourers who could meet the needs of industrial capitalism. In short, protecting workers from unscrupulous money-lenders was protecting them from their own worse selves so that they might go on to fulfill the productive roles open to them in the industrial armies that had come to characterize capitalism.

Driving out overt usurers did not, it must be pointed out, at first do much to change the financial position of the working-class, a majority of whom continued to remain at near subsistence wage levels in the early twentieth century.[11] Rather, it was ultimately the welfare state, itself predicated in important ways on the growth of a productivist regime geared to mass consumption, that led to the relative decline of predatory lenders by midcentury. For example, A. L. Minkes, a British student of the phenomenon of pawnbroking, explained its comparative decline in post-war Britain as largely determined by that country's commitment to a full-employment economy: "The broad explanations of the decreased importance of pawnbroking are, on the demand side, the great extension of the scope of social policy, the maintenance of continued full employment, and changes in the opportunities and attitudes of consumers, and on the supply side, the declining relative attractiveness of pawnbroking as an occupation".[12]

It is in this second variant of liberal governance, manifested in the growth of the welfare state, that one also witnessed an alteration in the underlying goal of the rhetoric of responsibilization directed at the working class. As is now generally acknowledged, the development of the welfare state decidedly did not entail a decommodification of labour, particularly in Anglo-American countries where its various programs were from the start modeled on an insurance logic and conceived as wage enhancement not replacement schemes.[13] In fact, one of the effects of this insurance-styled welfare state was that it allowed for a more orderly process of entry into, and exit from, the labour market, hence supplying capital with a more predictable and knowable workforce intimately tied to the corporate economic order and new state structure that were being constructed by the mid-twentieth century. In his recent work on the intersecting rhetoric of social and national security that began to appear in U.S. political and economic discourse during the Roosevelt administration and in the immediate post-WWII years, Neocleous points out how its underlying theme of insecurity worked to help restructure social order around the needs of corporate capital.[14] Admonitions about social insurance as protection against the economic vagaries of life reinforced the idea that economic insecurity is an enduring condition of working life which can never be disposed of, only allayed by fidelity to the capitalist order that underwrites the financial stability of welfare state capitalism. By the same measure, national security increasingly became portrayed as the *modus vivendi* for economic security, prompting both the expansion of an ever more integrated military-industrial complex and an all-embracing security-identity-loyalty complex.

Powerful as these rhetorical tropes were in establishing the ideological outline of the second variant of liberal governance, tangible transformations in the economic prospects of a majority of workers were crucial in the integration of the working class to the capitalist order with its new internalized rules of behaviour. For together with an emergent high wage economy in certain industrial sectors and the episodic deployment of demand management macroeconomic policies, state welfare provisioning did help make possible the mass consumption society that marked the second variant of modern liberal governance. In this second variant, the production of cultural norms of consumption, and the participation of the working class in this moveable feast now emblematic of industrial mass production, came to characterize capitalism, especially in its dynamic centre, the U.S. in the immediate post-WWII era. With the growth of a mass consumption economy, a new kind of financial discipline was required of workers. No longer were they exhorted to save enough from their near subsistence wages to tide themselves through the bad times; now instead they were enticed to purchase through newly created forms of credit those durable goods that signified a suitably fabricated cultural status.[15] Establishing and maintaining credit-worthiness thus became both a goal of, and a means of social control over, workers during the golden age of consumer capitalism. Self-responsibilization now meant exhibiting the kind of financial reliability that would entitle one to take out mortgages, and car and appliance loans, and carry on with the payments until the debts were discharged.

But just as it became the hegemonic political form of liberalism, the welfare state's ability to contain the contradictions inhering in capitalist production began to be severely tested. In response to recurrent profitability crises in latter part of the twentieth century, compounded by high inflation and high unemployment for which the term 'stagflation' was coined, governments in developed capitalist nations began the historic transition from Keynesian to neo-liberal economic policies. While the consequences of this neo-liberal turn for welfare state policy has been exhaustively canvassed,[16] its impact on the institutions of working class credit has received comparatively less attention. Yet it is in this sphere of personal economic life that one can see in a remarkably clear way the contours of a new security discourse that presently is supplanting the social/national security diptych associated with the twentieth century welfare state.

Symptomatic of this changing discourse are both the phenomenon of modern payday lending and the various state policies introduced to regulate it. While payday lending had virtually disappeared in advanced capitalist economies because of the increased state supervision of credit markets in the early twentieth century coupled with the growth of working class income associated in part with welfare provisioning, its resurfacing in the U.S. and elsewhere in last decade of the twentieth century signaled not only the extent to which incomes were declining but also the social and institutional effects of the state deregulation of financial industries. In fact the latter had a direct bearing on the return of payday lending as an everyday facet of life among an increasingly larger segment of the working poor.

Payday lending first began reappearing in check-cashing outlets in the U.S. in the early 1990s. Check-cashing facilities were themselves a relatively modern phenomenon that arose in Chicago and New York in the 1930s just as it became more commonplace for workers to receive their wages in the form of a cheque rather than a pay packet, and as welfare entitlements began to appear, again in the form of periodic cheques. Cheque cashers set up shop in certain districts in these cities because regular banks elected not to service them for reasons of their racial, ethnic and socio-economic composition. By the 1970's and 1980's the desertion by banks of ever larger numbers of impoverished neighborhoods led to such a dramatic proliferation of cheque cashing stores that they became a familiar feature of the North American urban landscape.[17] Meanwhile, pressures began to mount on governments to repeal or alter their legislation governing small loans and usurious practices because the high interest rate policy of central banks during the 1980s, aimed at combating inflation, had the effect on making commercial as well as consumer loans not only more expensive but potentially illegal. Britain was one of the first countries to succumb to calls for the deregulation of interest rates by abandoning its 48% ceiling on interest charges in the 1974 Consumer

Credit Act. In the United States a majority of state governments likewise amended their Small Loan Acts in the 1980s to allow for higher interest charges, while in Canada, Parliament followed the British lead by partially deregulating interest rates in 1980. Because of concerns voiced by the Montreal police force about the prevalence of criminal loan-sharking in that city, a provision was added to the Canadian criminal code defining as usurious and hence illegal interest charges above 60% per annum, the net effect of which was to make anything below that limit a legally acceptable market rate.[18]

It was in the U.S., however, with the peculiarities of its complex jurisdictional division of powers over finance, that the modern business of payday lending initially developed out of the neo-liberal movement to deregulate credit. A catalytic event that set the stage for the renaissance of payday lending was a court ruling—*Marquette National Bank of Minnesota v. First of Omaha Service Corp et al*—where it was decided that national lenders could charge common interest rates in all states. The practical consequence of this ruling was that lending institutions with a national presence, intent on escaping remaining stringent state laws on interest charges, could simply choose the expedient of incorporating in a state with high or no interest rate ceilings.[19] Alternatively, local lenders could affiliate with federally-regulated banks, thereby circumventing their own state laws on lending rates. In either case the result in the United States was a setting loose of interest rates similar to what obtained in the U.K. after its 1974 Consumer Credit Act. In this new deregulated environment, cheque cashing companies began to offer payday loans and started to spread nationally with the collusion of a handful of banks who effectively "rented" to them the charter powers they had gained under the *Marquette* doctrine.[20] Within a span of a decade and a half payday lending exploded. In the early 1990s it was estimated that there were only around 200 payday businesses operating throughout the U.S.; by 2006 the number of payday lenders nation-wide exceeded the number of Macdonalds and Burger King locations.[21] The value of the short term loans made by these companies has been estimated at a staggering $25 billion by 2003, double the level it had reached at the beginning of the new millennium.[22] This American phenomenon was in turn exported abroad to Canada and Britain where payday operations multiplied in the last decade at a similar hurried pace. Again, starting from a only handful of facilities in the mid-1990s, there appeared in Canada by 2004 at least 1350 such outlets—rivaling the number of Royal Bank of Canada branches—with payday lending worth an estimated $1.7 billion.[23] Britain experienced a comparable rapid increase in payday lending during this same period, as evidenced, for example, by the growth of The Money Shop, a subsidiary of the U.S. market leader, Dollar Financial. The Money Shop expanded from one location in 1992 to 273 stores and 64 franchises across the U.K. in 2009.[24] In that country it has been estimated that the industry as a whole made about £1.2 billion worth of loans in 2009, generating gross revenues of £242 million worth more than 20% of the total lent.[25]

Enormous as these revenues and profit levels are, it must be kept in mind that payday lending is only one part of a larger subprime financial market that includes everything from check cashing, prepaid credit cards, automobile title loans, leaseback loans, injury loans, and, of course, the infamous mortgages which precipitated the current financial crisis starting with the liquidity breakdown in U.S. banks. This subprime credit market has not only become a significant component of the financial services market, but it increasingly is a sector to which mainstream financial institutions are drawn. This is true not only of U.S. subprime mortgages but also of the outlier segments of this market like payday lending, which, as recent studies have shown, rely more and more on traditional banks for their loan capital.[26] This interlacing of mainsteam and subprime financial markets, at least to the extent evident today, is a novel development in modern capitalism, and, as shall presently be argued, is an indication of the kind of economy that underlies the shift to that third variant of liberal governance that is coming to be engraved in the present-day security discourse. To appreciate what is involved in this transformation it is necessary first to consider the ways in which subprime lenders like payday loan companies target their market and the measures they take to ensure their profits.

"The payday advance service is a cost-efficient 'financial taxi' to get from one payday to another when a consumer is faced with a small, short-term cash need", advises the Community Financial Services Association of America, the U.S. payday lenders' professional association.[27] In their promotional literature, sponsored studies or submissions to legislative committees, payday lenders constantly recur to the same proposition: a payday loan is an occasional service made use of by individuals of all income levels because it is a convenient, expedient and comparatively inexpensive way of solving short-term insolvency. Yet every reputable study has shown this proposition to be false. Claims of it being a class-neutral resource, for example, have been belied by location analyses which conclusively show that payday lenders in the U.S. concentrate their outlets in poor working class districts.[28] More fine-grained analyses have revealed that these lenders increasingly favour racially segregated neighborhoods.[29] And in a final ironic twist, in an age in which national security has almost entirely displaced the social security half of contemporary security discourse, a recent survey has shown that payday lenders have found it profitable to reinvent themselves as modern-day sutlers, choosing the immediate environs of military bases as a preferred location for setting up business.[30] With poverty the observable tie that binds these several "customer" bases of payday lending, the mechanisms of ensuring profits are likewise obvious despite protestations to the contrary by industry spokespersons. The latter, using the rhetoric of responsible lending, insist that they abide by a code of conduct that precludes them from trying to trap borrowers in endless cycles of debt.[31] But again study after study has demonstrated that ensnaring borrowers in debt traps is precisely what drives the profit levels for payday lenders.[32]

Given assorted charges that amount to an annual percentage rate of over 400% for these loans, compounded by the fact that borrowers average 8-13 loans per year,[33] and it is easy to understand why payday lending has become such a rapidly growing industry. Also not surprising is the fact that, much as was the case in the early twentieth century, various and sundry movements have arisen to fight against extortionate lending to the poor. While state measures that have resulted from these mobilizations against payday lending have varied considerably in the Anglo-American world surveyed in this chapter, there has recently emerged three broad patterns: banning payday lending outright; limiting the rates they can charge for their loans; and requiring firms to disclose to customers the true cost of their loans in a more accessible manner. With comparatively few jurisdictions having successfully implemented a total ban on payday lending, regulatory reform has generally meant some combination of rate capping and truth-in-lending requirements. To get a sense of both the practical and ideological implications of such regulatory reform, it is instructive to consider briefly the Canadian case because the manner in which a national policy on payday lending was reached in that country exemplifies the triumph of a new form of liberal governance.

Prior to 2007, payday lending in Canada escaped virtually all government regulation because it fell between the jurisdictional cracks. Since they were not deposit-taking institutions, payday lending firms were not subject to federal financial laws. And although their activities fell under provincial consumer protection laws, the latter generally had little to say about financial instruments. Finally, although Canada did retain a usury section in its criminal code making interest charges above 60% liable to prosecution, this provision was never used by state officials for fear that its enforcement would lead to a slippery slope where legitimate short term commercial financial arrangements would also be found to be illegal. Mounting pressures from consumers' advocates did eventually force federal and provincial governments to take heed of the growing opposition to predatory lending, and a process was set in train in 2002 to come up with a politically acceptable regulatory regime. A consultative process was established involving both federal and provincial officials, together with payday loan company representatives and consumer advocacy groups, to devise a regulatory framework for the industry. What was noteworthy about this consultative process was the logic of choice that it embraced in it deliberations. The growth of the payday lending business, it was conceded from the start, indicated a strong consumer demand for the products they provide. Outlawing this business outright might channel this demand to illegal quarters. Employing coercive state measures to try to force mainstream financial institutions to replicate the existing payday loan industry would run counter to free market principles, as would pursuing an incomes policy in an effort to minimize the demand for short-term credit. In such circumstances what remained as a policy option was some combination of consumer protection and education measures that would eliminate some of the more conspicuous exploitative practices associated with the industry while providing loan recipients with the information necessary to make informed choices. And given Canada's federal division of responsibilities for consumer protection, it would be necessary for the provinces to take the lead in this latter kind of regulatory initiative.

It was this kind of calculation which eventually led the federal government to devolve to the provinces the responsibility for regulating payday lending, in the process specifically exempting these companies from any future application of the criminal law sanction against usury so long as provinces developed some sort of rules that protected recipients of payday loans and placed limits on the total cost of borrowing. Such vague conditions meant that that the substantive regulatory battles have been taking place in the provinces as their governments began assuming their regulatory assignment.[34] What was never in serious doubt in these regulatory fights, however, was the continued existence of a payday loan industry. For in almost all instances provincial regulatory debates in the years since 2007 have followed a basic script laid down by the original bureaucratic consultative body that had spelled out the logic of choice facing policy-makers. Any prospective laws governing payday lending, that consultative body insisted, had to respect two imperatives: "(1) Regulation – how to best foster and ensure an 'alternative' credit industry which can provide services to consumers who cannot or do not use traditional sources of financing for their short term credit needs. (2) Education – how to make consumers aware of the relative costs and implications of borrowing in [this market]".[35]

This frank assertion about the dual policy imperatives that any regulations of the payday loan industry must satisfy perfectly captures the spirit of the third variant of liberal governance now upon us. First there is the ordering of these policy imperatives: government's primary responsibility it turns out is to create conditions *favourable* to the flourishing of the payday loan industry so they can provide the poor with short term credit. And second, governments must ensure that there is enough transparency in the lending process so that it can be presumed that loan-takers are making informed choices when taking out these loans. This latter policy goal of transparency fixes on loan-takers the responsibility for their credit choices, thus making the poor accountable for whatever debt traps they might thereby experience. While this self-responsibilization gambit might seem a reiteration of the original liberal project of the late nineteenth and early twentieth century aimed at embedding in workers an appropriate financial discipline, there are enough unique features in the contemporary political vocabulary of personal accountability to think that it signifies a different governance objective.

The first variant of liberal governance advocated personal financial responsibility as part of a larger moralization undertaking meant to fashion a working class that was reliable and hence functional to the process of creating surplus value that is at the heart of capitalist enterprise. Once fordist-styled production and Keynesian-inspired economic policy became the norm in capitalism, a second variant of liberal governance arose that stressed the need for workers to exhibit sound management of personal finances so that they could continually consume the products of their labour, thereby contributing to the process of capital accumulation and reproduction. But the historic turn to neo-liberal economic policies in the late twentieth century set in motion changes in the organization and distribution of capitalist enterprise that rendered the working class not only more vulnerable to job losses or a restructured work environment, but also made its capacity to consume less directly connected to a flourishing national bourgeoisie. During the height of the Keynesian compromise, a consuming working class was one of the conditions of existence of domestically-geared mass production. State economic policies were at the time designed to abet this particular model of capital accumulation by helping sustain relatively closed economies in which demand management strategies could help ensure a sufficient level of domestic consuming power, especially in the form of a relatively affluent working class. The new internationalized industrial supply chain and attendant global division of labour which neo-liberalism has helped usher in has meant that the social and institutional foundations for Keynesian domestic stimulatory policies have been more-or-less been undermined. So to the extent that a nation's working class no longer figures as an important source of demand fueling domestic growth, its place in the capitalist order reverts to the role of producing surplus value *simpliciter*. Hence the neo-liberal impetus to once again reduce the costs to capital of labour, including whatever social costs are borne by the state.

In this rush to return to the nineteenth century, older tropes of self-responsibilzation have been dusted off and put in service to remind workers that they must be prepared to look after their own welfare. But what is different about this discourse in the twenty-first century is that just as more and more workers are becoming marginal or surplus to the needs of capitalist production in advanced capitalist societies, a new breed of rentier capitalist has discovered their ready potential as a source of profit, not as producers of surplus value but as consumers of credit. These purveyors of credit to the working poor are no longer, as in the nineteenth century, minor figures in the world of finance, eventually to be swept away by regulation and a rising affluence. They are now becoming so central to modern economies that just prior to the financial crisis which originated in the U.S. banking sector, it was estimated that in countries like Briatin and the U.S. the subprime financial market comprised 30% of the overall retail lending market.[36] This statistic throws into sharp relief the evolving shape of liberal governance. Persuaded that unrelenting competition in the global marketplace requires them to moderate their wage demands and reconsider their expectations of a compensatory social wage, induced to believe that threats to national security by enemies unseen are now always imminent, the working class is at the same time instructed to read carefully the terms of its indebtedness and take ownership of its economic fate.

It is against this backdrop of the increasing immiseration of segments of the working-class, who have ended up resorting to virtually the same credit devices upon which their nineteenth century forbears had relied, that policy debates surrounding payday lending can be seen to contribute their own disciplining note to the ascendant security discourse of the twenty-first century. The very measures state agents have devised ostensibly to protect the working poor from exploitation by unscrupulous payday lenders underscore while simultaneously trying to disguise the systematic exploitation this population experiences by virtue of their class location. These measures, whether consisting of rate caps or truth-in-lending requirements, have the effect of legitimizing the payday lending industry and conferring on it all the legal and institutional advantages of the administrative state. One such advantage of this administrative arrangement is that the legal status of payday loans as voluntary contracts is confirmed, making loan-takers subject to the usual array of legal sanctions in case of default. State regulation in this instance supports the perpetual insecurity associated with penury, all the while offering to the working poor the banal admonition that resisting debt is the preferable course of action. It is in this prosaic way that the state helps procure the bawdy relationship between gold and want, helping both to normalize a new form of debt bondage while using the specter of this burden as a valuable cautionary tale for the internal governance of the working poor.

Notes

1 See OECD, *Growing Unequal? Income Distribution and Poverty in OECD Countries* (Paris: OECD, 2008).
2 Karl Polanyi, *The Great Transformation* (Boston: Beacon Press, 1957), Mitchell Dean, *The Constitution of Poverty: Toward a Genealogy of Liberal Governance* (London: Routledge, 1991), Mark Neocleous, *Administering Civil Society: Toward a Theory of State Power* (Houndmills, U.K.: Macmillan Press, 1996) and *The Fabrication of Social Order: A Critical Theory of Police Power* (London: Pluto Press, 2000).
3 Neocleous, *Fabrication of Social Order*.
4 This is a theme that appears prominently in Dean, *The Constitution of Poverty*, Neocleous, *Fabrication of Social Order*; James Dickinson and Bob Russell, *Family, Economy and State: the Social Reproduction Process Under Capitalism* (Halifax: Garamond, 1986); Paul Corrigan and Peter Leonard, *Social Work Practice under Capitalism* (London: Macmillan, 1978); Heide Gerstenberger, 'The Poor and the Respectable Worker: On the Introduction of Social Insurance in Germany', *Labour History*, Vol. 48, 1985, pp. 69-85; and Frances Fox Piven and Richard A. Cloward, *Regulating the Poor: The Functions of Public Welfare* (London: Tavistock, 1972).
5 Graham Burchell, 'Liberal Government and Techniques of the Self' in Andrew Barry, Thomas Osborne and Nikolas Rose (eds.), *Foucault and Political Reason* (London: UCL Press, 1996).
6 Steven M. Graves and Christopher L. Peterson, 'Predatory Lending and the Military: The Law and Geography of "Payday" Loans in Military Towns', *Ohio State Law Journal*, Vol. 66, No. 4, 2005, pp. 653-832.
7 Mark H. Haller and John V. Alviti, 'Loansharking in American Cities: Historical Analysis of a Marginal Enterprise', *American Journal of Legal History*, Vol. 21, No. 2, 1977, pp. 125-156.
8 Sean O'Connell, *Credit and Community Working-Class Debt in the UK Since 1880* (Oxford: Oxford University Press, 2009).
9 Rolf Nugent, 'The Loan Shark Problem', *Law and Contemporary Problems*, Vol. 8, No. 3, 1941, pp. 3-23, p. 6.
10 Mary E. Richmond, *Friendly Visiting Among the Poor: A Handbook for Charity Workers* (London: Macmillan, 1907), pp. 111-112.
11 Frank Stricker, 'Affluence for Whom? Another Look at Affluence and the Working Class in the 1920s', *Labor History*, Vol. 24, No. 1, 1983, pp. 5-33.

12 A.L.Minkes, 'The Decline of Pawnbroking', *Economica*, Vol. 20, February 1953, pp. 10-23, p. 21.
13 Gosta Esping-Andersen, *The Three Worlds of Welfare Capitalism* (Cambridge: Polity Press, 1990).
14 Mark Neocleous, *Critique of Security* (Edinburgh: Edinburgh University Press, 2008).
15 See Lendol Calder, *Financing the American Dream: A Cultural History of Consumer Credit* (Princeton: Princeton University Press, 1999) and Sheryl Kroen, 'A Political History of the Consumer', *The Historical Journal*, Vol. 47, No. 3, 2004, pp. 709-736.
16 See, for example, Andrew Glyn, *Capitalism Unleashed: Finance, Globalization and Welfare* (Oxford: Oxford University Press, 2007); Jacob S. Hacker, 'Privatizing Risk without Privatizing the Welfare State: The Hidden Politics of Social Policy Retrenchment in the United States', *American Political Science Review*, Vol. 98, No. 22, 2004, pp. 243–60, Bob Jessop, 'Towards a Schumpeterian Workfare State? Preliminary Remarks on Post-Fordist Political Economy', *Studies in Political Economy*, Vol. 40, 1993, pp. 7-40, and Ramesh Mishra, *Globalization and the Welfare State* (Cheltenham, U.K.: Edward Elgar Publishing, 1999).
17 See John Caskey, *Fringe Banking: Check-Cashing Outlets, Pawnshops, and the Poor* (New York: Russell Sage Foundation, 1994).
18 Mary-Anne Waldron, *The Law of Interest in Canada.* (Scarborough, Ont.: Carswell, 1992).
19 The advantages of locating in states with no or extremely high interest rate ceilings was not lost on the U.S. credit card companies after the Marquette decision as witnessed by the current location of the top ten credit card issuers: Citibank (South Dakota, no interest rate ceiling); American Express (Utah, no interest rate ceiling); Bank of America (Arizona, 36% interest rate ceiling); Providian (New Hampshire, no interest rate ceiling); JP Morgan Chase, MBNA, Morgan Stanley, HSBC (Delaware, no interest rate ceiling); and Capital One (Virginia, no interest rate ceiling). Information gathered from "Secret History of the Credit Card." *PBS Frontline.* http://www.pbs.org/wgbh/pages/frontline/shows/credit/ - accessed February 18, 2011.
20 Elizabeth R. Schiltz, 'The Amazing, Elastic, Ever-Expanding Exportation Doctrine and Its Effect on Predatory Lending Regulation', *Minn. Law Review*, Vol. 88, 2004, pp. 518-540.

21 Caskey, *Fringe Banking*. See also Gary Rivlin, *From Pawnshops to Poverty, Inc.—How the Working Poor Became Big Business* (New York: HarperCollins Publishers, 2010).
22 Keith Ernst, John Farris and Uriah King, *Quantifying the Economic Cost of Predatory Payday Lending* (Durham, N.C.: Center for Responsible Lending, 2004).
23 Wade Hemsworth, 'Quick Cash: Payday loans are a $1.7-billion unregulated industry', *Hamilton Spectator*, April 15, 2006, A01.
24 Damon Gibbons, Neha Malhotra, and Richard Bulmore, *Payday Lending in the UK: a Review of the Debate and Policy Options* (London: Centre for Responsible Credit, 2010.)
25 Marie Burton, *Keeping the plates spinning. Perceptions of payday loans in Great Britain.* (London: Consumer Focus, 2010.)
26 Kevin Connor, and Matthew Skomarovsky, *The Predators' Creditors. How the Biggest Banks are Bankrolling the Payday Loan Industry* (Chicago: National People's Action and Public Accountability Initiative, 2009) - http://showdowninamerica.org/files/payday-final-091410.pdf accessed February 20, 2011.
27 Community Financial Association Services of America (CFSA), *Is A Payday Advance Appropriate For You?* 2011 - http://www.cfsaa.com/ourresources/What Is a PaydayAdvance/IsaPaydayAdvanceAppropriateForYou.aspx - accessed March 11, 2011.
28 Steven Graves, 'Landscapes of Predation, Landscapes of Neglect: A Location
Analysis of Payday Lenders and Banks', *Professional Geographer*, Vol. 55, 2003, 303-317.
29 See Nicholas Bianchi, *Credit Segregation: Concentrations of Predatory Lenders in Communities of Color* (Chicago: National People's Action, 2011) and Wei Li, Leslie Parrish, Keith Ernst and Delvin Davis, *Predatory Profiling: The Role of Race and Ethnicity in the Location of Payday Lenders in California* (Oakland, Calif.: Center for Responsible Lending, 2009.)
30 Graves and Peterson, 'Predatory Lending'.
31 See Community Financial Association Services of America (CFSA), *CFSA Member Best Practices*, 2011 - http://www.cfsaa.com/CFSAMemberBestPractices.aspx accessed March 11, 2011 and Canadian Payday Loan Association (CPLA), *Code of Best Business Practices*, 2011 http://www.cpla-acps.ca/english/consumercode.php - accessed March 11, 2011.

Anti-Security
Edited by Mark Neocleous and
George Rigakos

32 See Michael A. Stegman and Robert Faris, 'Payday Lending: A Business Model that Encourages Chronic Borrowing', *Economic Development Quarterly*, Vol. 17, 2003, pp. 8-32; Howard Jacob Karger, *Shortchanged: Life and Debt in the Fringe Economy* (San Francisco: Berrett-Koehler, 2005); and Henry Palmer with Pat Conaty, *Profiting from Poverty. Why Debt is Big Business in Britain* (London: New Economics Foundation 2002).
33 Ernst et al, *Quantifying the Economic Cost*.
34 For a fuller account of this political history, consult Olena Kobzar, 'Perils of Governance through Networks: The Case of Regulating Payday Lending in Canada', *Law and Policy* (forthcoming 2011).
35 Alternative Consumer Credit Working Group of the Consumer Measures Committee (ACCWG), *Consultation Paper on Framework Options For Addressing Concerns With The Alternative Consumer Credit Market*, (Ottawa: Industry Canada, 2002) http://cmcweb.ca/eic/site/cmc-cmc.nsf/eng/fe00025.html - accessed February 14, 2011.
36 Sinclair Stewart, 'Big banks target sub-prime lenders; TD latest buyer, snaps up VFC', *The Globe and Mail*, 17 February 2006, B1.

[6]

Liberal Intellectuals and the Politics of Security

WILL JACKSON

To mount a critique of the current politics of security it is essential to understand how the logic of security has become seemingly impenetrable. If we follow Marx in understanding security as *the supreme concept of bourgeois society* we should not be surprised that the capitalist state reveals itself to be increasingly enamoured with the concept. Yet in the current epoch the saturation of the political and social landscape with the logic of security is not solely a result of the state's increasingly clear obsession but has been greatly affected by the rapid and unfailing expansion of the intellectual engagement with security.

We are aware that the events of 9/11 did not mark the beginning of this security obsession and also aware that the state drawing legitimacy from intellectuals is not a new observation.[1] However, there has arguably been an intensification of the relationship between intellectuals and security politics in the last decade influenced most explicitly by the unrivalled expansion of 'security studies'. While this essentially conservative discipline has by virtue of its own fetishization of security served only to reinforce the concerns of the state[2] (a practice that pre-dates 2001), there is a need to look beyond this specialism to consider the broader influence of the intellectual in relation to the politics of security.

In order to fully appreciate the role of the intellectual in this context there is a need to develop an understanding of the current regime or more specifically, an understanding of the *presentation* of this regime and its place in a liberal democracy. The concept of security in the current era is inextricably bound up with the discourse of human rights and this has given rise to a *liberty-security regime* within which the idea of security is seemingly inseparable from concerns about the preservation of liberty. The relationship between liberty and security is not a new concern for the liberal but the expansion of the 'war on terror' has lead to a return to this central dynamic within liberal circles inciting much debate on the appropriate and effective simultaneous accommodation of both concerns. The resulting debate has incited innumerable commentaries seeking to critically analyse the current regime and revisit the liberal formulation of security vis-à-vis liberty – with liberty in this sense predominantly, if not exclusively, couched in the language of human rights.

There has been a deluge of ostensibly critical liberal interventions predicated on the idea that the current politics of security are illiberal due to their disproportionate emphasis on security. These intellectuals seek in response to dictate an alternate, liberal approach of security in relation to human rights that reinstates a vision of liberalism defined by the prioritisation of liberty over security. However, since this intellectual intervention, broadly conceived, remains committed to and defined by liberalism it is, in Peter Hallward's conceptualisation, tied ultimately to an intellectual stance of alignment with the world as it is.[3] In this sense these liberal intellectuals are aligned with the dominant ideology and their position is characterised by an acceptance of all that really matters. The idea of alignment with or acceptance of the world, that is to say, of the status quo, appears - by seemingly confirming the insubstantial nature of a liberal critique of the liberal state - to render the liberal intellectual an easy target for critique. However, this critique may also be 'easy', except when, which is not often the case, it grasps the actual, invaluable service the liberal intelligentsia renders to the current liberty-security regime and, more generally, to the status quo. That the liberal intellectual fulfils a decisive function in relation to the politics of security is quite obvious. Much less obvious is the precise nature of this function, the way in which it is performed and the far-reaching consequences of it. For such liberal 'critique' may actually be a critique only in appearance and may fulfil legitimising functions which can only be fulfilled in the form of a critique or the semblance of it.

This paper understands security to be a fully political concept and its first contention is that the liberal intellectual intervention in the security arena has not simply been a reaction to the current politics of security, but is instead bound up in the formulation and subsequent legitimisation of the current security regime. Secondly, I wish to suggest that the liberal critique of security politics plays a decisive legitimising function of the current liberty-security regime; it is a conservative function in relation to the status quo, but one which cannot be played by the more conservative or straight supporters of such security politics. Thirdly, the paper seeks to point toward the convergence between the liberal intelligentsia's views on security and the position of the state. Finally, it seeks to provide an initial analysis of the consequences of the liberal intervention. Taking into account that a devastating process of depoliticisation has been shown to be a major consequence of human rights promotion and activism, the paper is above all concerned with the potential depoliticising effects that may be borne out of the liberal contribution to a debate that is at once premised on human rights advocacy and conducted on a political terrain defined by liberalism.

At the core of the paper there is a concern with what it actually means to be a liberal intellectual in concrete terms and what this suggests for an alternative intellectual project able to politicise security and radically question the logic of current security politics.

The security compromise

The liberty-security debate has included interventions from leading liberal intellectuals including Michael Ignatieff, Michael Walzer, Ronald Dworkin and Richard Rorty whose contributions have arguably been incited by the human rights advocacy central to their work. I wish to illustrate, by way of a focus on these four public intellectuals, that they both embody the central tenets of the liberal intellectual position on the current politics of security and precisely because of that, play a pivotal role in (re)defining them in the current, allegedly new, situation of the 'war against terror'. There are of course many other academics, scholars, journalists, analysts and commentators who potentially perform the same function as intellectuals in the Gramscian sense but the role of this public intellectual 'strata' needs to be set out to illustrate the specific effect it has had on defining the parameters for debate on the liberty-security relationship, and by extension, the parameters for any critical discussion of the politics of security.

The approach to the current liberty-security relationship is based (for the four intellectuals in focus here and numerous others) in an agreement that the 'war on terror' has distorted the equilibrium that is the central characteristic of liberalism. The first marker of the essentially shared position between these intellectuals is agreement that the defining feature of the current era is an unavoidable confrontation with a set of opposing concerns. There is disagreement on which concerns are the most relevant and pressing but all four are united in their agreement that the concept of balance provides the appropriate framework for the necessary reestablishment of the central equilibrium. Ignatieff and Walzer predictably confront largely the same set of requirements – ultimately liberty and security – and seek to articulate the appropriate liberal balance between these two. Dworkin and Rorty are not so explicit in their approach to the liberty-security dynamic but are both in agreement that balance is the framework that liberalism dictates. Ultimately, these intellectuals are incapable of operating outside the balance metaphor as it is the liberal response *par excellence* to any set of opposing concerns.[4]

The idea of striking a balance is further entrenched in the proposals made by all four intellectuals through their agreement that the response to terrorism must follow a 'third model' or 'middle way' between alternatives – that is clearly a variant of the balance metaphor. Ignatieff's *Lesser Evil* (2005) perspective and Walzer's return to *Just War Theory* (2004) both frame this 'middle way' essentially between left and right crudely defined for them by pacifism and realism respectively. Dworkin and Rorty seek to define a 'third model' but focus rather on the unsuitability of both the 'war' and 'crime' models of response to terrorism. A concern with the seemingly novel policing function of the 'war on terror' is indeed a point of convergence for all four intellectuals. In Rorty's words the threat in this period to 'civilisation' comes from people who "were not exactly enemy combatants and not exactly criminals"[5] and thus necessitates an alternative model of response. The construction of the liberal response as in some way a departure from both war and policing serves only to mystify the nature of security.

The politics of the liberal intelligentsia is essentially a politics of compromise, assuming a shared understanding of the political terrain, which on Ignatieff's terms is opposed directly to terrorism understood to be a "form of politics that aims at the death of politics itself"[6]. For Ignatieff, terrorism is ultimately apolitical as it refuses to conform to the politics of deliberation and compromise, which, in a true liberal fashion, he posits as the only basis for a sound politics. In development of this idea Walzer suggests that the terrorism faced by the west in the current era is distinct from the terrorism fought in the past premised as it is not on ideas of fighting for freedom but on *jihad* that for Walzer is characterised comprehensively by a "fundamentalist religious response to modernity".[7]

The emphasis on jihad as the defining backdrop for international terrorism illustrates Walzer's acceptance that contemporary terrorism is characterised not only exclusively by religion but more specifically by a synonymous affiliation with Islam. This position shared by Walzer and those liberal states at the forefront of the 'war on terror' is at the very core of the dominant discourse on 'international terrorism' and points to what Wendy Brown has termed the "culturalization of politics",[8] that constitutes one of the most significant "discourses of depoliticisation" in contemporary liberal democracies.[9]

The construction of the 'war on terror' as a legitimate project builds on the justifications for humanitarian intervention found in Ignatieff's earlier work. Much of his work has been devoted to opening up a space to justify such action as well as the inevitable 'collateral damage' within the liberal framework. Actually, in *The Lesser Evil* he develops this 'ethics of intervention' justifying the 'war on terror' on the basis of the same moralising approach. Justifying the resort to the most extreme action (as humanitarian interventions always involve) as a 'lesser evil' is ultimately possible because Ignatieff's position embodies the active subject of human rights[10]. This places him on the 'right side' in the battle between good and evil that frames the politics of humanitarian intervention and in the same sense, frames the 'war on terror'.

This binary opposition between 'good' and 'evil' is at the core of the depoliticised moralising framework of human rights that defines the 'Lesser Evil' perspective. Brown has suggested that human rights in Ignatieff's work "take their shape as a moral discourse centred on pain and suffering rather than political discourse of comprehensive justice".[11] The emphasis is on the suffering of the individual and as opposed to suggesting an alternative formulation of justice all collective justice projects are seemingly dismissed as utopian – the protection of human rights is in Ignatieff's words "the most we can hope for".[12]

This reinforces Badiou's warning that in the contemporary 'ethics' of human rights "every collective will to the Good" is seen to "create Evil".[13] Furthermore, Ignatieff's approach to human rights involves a reduction of their remit to simply "a decidedly 'thin' theory of what is right, a definition of the minimum conditions for any kind of life at all".[14] This reduction of human rights activism to the preservation only of what resembles Agamben's 'bare life' illustrates that for Ignatieff the passive subject of human rights – the focus of his humanitarian 'concern' – is, as Badiou has noted, defined by its "subhumanity, by bare biological or animal life". Both Ignatieff and Walzer's interventions are rooted in the moralising approach that characterises liberal politics and defines the liberal state's approach to security. The promotion of their proposals as being defined by regulation is in reality yet another mobilisation of the liberal pretence of restraint that attempts to deny not only the reality of war but the fact that a 'just war' is a war uncontrolled in its violence.

Neutralisation and depoliticisation

While there is some degree of separation between Ignatieff/Walzer and Dworkin/Rorty based on the extent of their explicit commitment to regulation, in terms of over-arching political framework the distinction is ultimately insubstantial. Dworkin and Rorty's total commitment to regulation is combined with the moralising and depoliticising approach to politics that characterises Ignatieff and Walzer. As a result Dworkin and Rorty's position provides an enhancement of the formal containment of the sovereign that is always at the core of liberal politics.

The depoliticisation at the core of Dworkin's approach renders the current status quo – of which the 'war on terror' is a prominent feature – effectively undisturbed. This approach is for Dworkin not limited to the response to terrorism and is at the core of his project of reinvigorating politics.[15] Dworkin's concern with the relationship between human rights and security is part of his broader concern with the 'war like' formulation of US politics in which conflict between the 'two cultures' of red and blue prevents 'shared principles' and political debate. Dworkin is explicit that liberalism should define the new politics – indeed liberal politics for Dworkin *is* politics – and the concept of shared humanity alongside a reaffirmation of liberal individualism should form the basis around which politics can be 'rejuvenated' and conflict denied.[16] It is in the context of this broader depoliticising project that his approach to the liberty-security relationship is situated.

Dworkin's function as an intellectual can be aligned with Ignatieff and Walzer to the extent that his articulation of the 'true' liberal response serves to reinforce the legitimacy of not only current security policies but also the broader political and economic arrangement. The reinvigoration of liberalism serves only to further marginalise and delegitimise conflict and deny any potential for truly alternative politics. The reformist strain in Dworkin and more clearly in Rorty's work does at least initially mark them apart from Ignatieff and Walzer but it is clear on further analysis that the marginalisation of conflict remains a process unaffected by reform.

Rorty's reformist project in relation to human rights was proposed prior to the era of the 'war on terror'[17] but understanding the thrust of these reforms illustrates much about his response to the post 9/11 security regime. His reformulation is not an attempt to transcend the human rights framework but to reconfigure the process by which this framework is 'sold' outside the Enlightenment tradition. His concern with the current response to terrorism lies more specifically with the potential this has to hold back the globalisation of the liberal democratic framework and the human rights principles so central to it.

The aim of promoting a Eurocentric human rights culture beyond the West amounts *de facto* to extending the essentially liberal depoliticised political framework. A sense of Enlightenment continues to be the reserve of the Westerner as there is a pivotal difference in the construction of a sense of identity between people in the West and those outside. For those "untouched by the European Enlightenment" their sense of identity is "bound up in a sense of who they are *not*"[18] and thus rooted in conflict. The concern with this sense of identity and the drive to rectify it is symptomatic of Rorty's fear of conflict which is rooted in his subscription to the moralism of the contemporary humanitarian ethics that his 'revised' approach to human rights is incapable of transcending. If "the moralist inevitably feels antipathy towards politics as a domain of open contestation for power and hegemony"[19] this is as clear in Rorty's essentially depoliticised framework as it is for Ignatieff, Walzer and Dworkin. The aim of the liberal intellectual is the neutralisation of conflict and this lies at the root of the pervasive depoliticisation evident in their work pre and post 9/11.

It is ultimately clear that Dworkin and Rorty contribute – in the same way as Ignatieff and Walzer – to the project of imposing formal regulation on the state that in turn paradoxically provides a sense of legitimacy to the same political and military project they seek ostensibly to resist. This two pronged contribution with its inherent contradiction serves to sustain the void between formal presentation and operation of the state. In converging with the position of those liberal states leading the 'war on terror' all four intellectuals serve to bolster this 'war' by offering a sense of legitimacy to the violence it employs.[20] This contradiction is seemingly implicit in what appears to be a shared understanding of the role of the liberal intellectual.

'There is no alternative': the conservatism of the critical liberal

At the core of the position of each of these intellectuals is a drive to legitimate and sustain the current political and economic conditions defined as they are by liberal democracy and free-market capitalism. A critical analysis of their work pre and post 9/11 illustrates that their function as intellectuals consists ultimately in upholding the conception of the world shared by the liberal state. This has continued post

9/11 in the form of a clear convergence with the liberal state around the necessity of a 'war on terror' and an agreement on the form it should take.

Illustrating the convergence between the liberal intellectual and the liberal state around the form and subsequent legitimacy of the 'war on terror', Walzer has been cited in the introduction to The *U.S. Army/Marine Corps Counterinsurgency Field Manual* (2007) for having "restored our ability to think clearly about war – including its legitimacy and its demands".[21] Walzer's intervention has despite his pretence of a critical analysis provided a pivotal source of legitimacy to the 'war on terror' that is at present the most explicit current manifestation of the logic of security. The liberal intellectual is in fact continually occupied in a process of helping the state to 'rethink' its approach to security ultimately allowing it to continually present violence and war in the guise of peace. If the 'war on terror' stands as the latest in a long line of code words for the "permanent *pacification* required in/of the bourgeois polity"[22] then the liberal intellectual serves only to reinforce the mystification of this process.

To further grasp the conservative function of the liberal intellectual it is crucial to understand that fundamentally, Ignatieff's articulation of the human rights project has been from its inception an attempt to provide "a political-economic account of what markets need to survive".[23] This attempt must be placed at the core of the liberal intellectual project: "the specific behaviours legitimated by Dworkin's theory (of human rights) are those which are made necessary by the immanent logic of capitalism during the current historical period".[24] It must be noted that the centrality of this human rights theory in the liberal intellectual response to security in no sense constitutes a deviation from the current politics of security. If security is the supreme concept of bourgeois society then it is entirely unsurprising that it is intertwined with the refrain of 'human rights' that is "nothing other than the ideology of modern liberal capitalism".[25] Indeed, the depoliticisation at the core of human rights is an integral component of the politics of security and the liberal intervention based as it is on human rights serves by definition to reinforce the mystification of the violence at its core.

Walzer and Rorty's engagement with the left – as well as Ignatieff's drive to remove any 'left tilt' and political ambition from human rights projects and Dworkin's attempt to neutralise political conflict – is premised on the attempt to maintain the status quo. For this to be possible political alternatives have to be marginalised and rendered illegitimate – no wonder then that the attempt to 'reform' or reconfigure the left be central to this project. Walzer has called for the formation of a 'decent' left that will be able to contribute to a 'serious debate' about security on the basis of its transcendence of any ideological framework. From this standpoint any critical perspective that rejects the liberal framework and instead locates itself on the left in truly emancipatory terms should be excluded from any debate on security. For Walzer a 'decent' left is one that is explicitly post-ideological and refuses to maintain the seemingly archaic and unhelpful distinctions between liberalism and the left. By way of illustration of this reformulation of the left, Walzer is a major signatory of the *Euston Manifesto*, a declaration of principles produced in the UK in 2006 by a group of academics, journalists, and activists who sought to respond to what they saw as widespread violations of leftist principles in the post-9/11 era. Through this manifesto the signatories sought to propose a "fresh political alignment" in which the (decent) left should "reach out, rather, beyond the socialist Left towards egalitarian liberals and others of unambiguous democratic commitment".[26]

Rorty has advocated similar 'reforms' based on his wish to dismantle the Marxist hold on leftist politics that is again at the root of a desire to abandon any distinction between liberalism and the left.[27] The unwillingness to accept – so the claim goes – the viability of capitalism and the cluttered vocabulary of words such as 'commodification' and 'ideology' are symptomatic of the redundancy of Marxism that renders the leftist-liberal distinction outmoded. It is vital to note here that for Rorty (and the liberal intellectual more generally) a rejection of the validity and legitimacy of capitalism is symptomatic of a dead politics. We have passed the end of history and must in this post-ideological age be willing to accept the seemingly self-evident logic of capitalism. Unsurprisingly, given what we know about security, any political project that resists the legitimacy of bourgeois society is rejected outright.

The apparent transcendence of an ideological 'age' and the substitution of ideology with a culturalization of politics is the central premise of this depoliticised approach to security that is defined by the liberal intellectual in the response to terrorism. Illustrating the influence and subsequent diffusion of this approach to 'alternative' politics, Walzer's 'disciples' have suggested that the current threat to security emanates not simply from the unquestionable threat of international (read Islamic) terrorism but also from another illiberal threat – that of the 'old left'. Those on the left that refuse in any form to accept the logic of security are lumped together under the banner of "excusers of terrorism and tyranny". The conflation of opposition to military intervention (more broadly to the politics of security) and terrorism is reinforced by the definition of the 'far left' as nihilists[28] echoing Ignatieff's definition of international terrorists as "apocalyptic nihilists".[29] A failure to engage in the debate on liberal terms constitutes a nihilism that is not only devoid of any meaningful contribution but is itself a threat to security.

The apparent leftist sympathy with authoritarian or terrorist regimes is underpinned by a "new authoritarian Marxism" that, under the leadership of Badiou and Zizek, proposes a 'terrorist' theory of the state.[30] This essentialist 'analysis' of the contemporary left unites all leftist anti-war (or anti 'war on terror') sentiment together to be readily dismissed. The fear of any truly alternate politics confirms that this 'fresh political alignment' offers only a reinstatement of the liberal framework. The 'decent left' cannot offer an alternative political alignment as it is unwilling to reject the politics of security. More pressingly, the dismissal of theories of the state that refuse to accept and shore up the logic of security as 'terrorist' takes the delegitimisation of alternative politics to its 'logical' conclusion. Any truly alternative politics that seeks to oppose the politics of security can expect the same treatment.

The liberal response to security reinforced by the 'decent left' is ultimately symptomatic of today's post-politics that serves fundamentally to "undermine the possibility of a proper political act" based as it is on the depoliticisation of economics[31]. This political stance instead creates the space for an avowedly apolitical response to the contemporary world including to the current security regime. The depoliticisation at the core of the liberal intellectual's intervention serves to further mystify the issue of war and its role at the heart of security. However, this must not be considered as an issue confined to the 'war on terror' as it is "a long-standing ideological feature of the global war of capital".[32] The liberal intelligentsia stands as the vanguard of liberal politics masking of the social war of capital through the depoliticisation that defines their intervention. The importance of human rights to the liberal intellectual project is based on their main effect being the "depoliticisation of politics itself"[33]. If we understand rights as having become in the current context "rewards for accepting the dominant order" and have the effect of "depoliticising conflict"[34] then their integral status in the politics of security is unsurprising.

Thus although the liberal intellectual's appeal to human rights would seem to place them at the other end of the political spectrum from the security intellectual, the appeal turns out to perform the same conservative function as the security intellectual's work. And yet, the precise legitimating function of liberal intellectual cannot be played by a straight defender of the current security regime. If we understand security studies to be "as far as could be imagined from the idea of critique"[35] then the liberal critique based on human rights is equally as distant. This is because they both occupy the same essentially liberal political terrain and both share the "central categories and key conceptions of power, subjectivity and knowledge" with the hegemonic powers.[36] The prioritisation of security above all else is categorically liberal but so too is the maintenance of a façade that posits liberty as the primary concern.

Ultimately the role of the liberal intellectual is to maintain this age old façade that posits liberty as the central concept in liberalism. The continued assertion that liberalism prioritises liberty over security is founded in the mythical distinction between Hobbes and Locke that attributes them (respectively) either side of the balance between security and liberty. It is crucial to understand that the utility of this concept of balance (inevitably the central tool for the liberal intellectuals) continues to be based in its ability to hide the fact that security is the supreme concept of liberal society.[37] A critical analysis that deconstructs this mystification must make clear that the politics of security are liberal politics and not some form of aberration or distortion. The attempt to define an alternate, truly liberal relation between liberty and security is not simply a fruitless task (from the point of view of any true alternative politics) but its dominance as the overarching goal of the liberal intellectual maintains the façade that is the crucial source of liberalism's perceived legitimacy.

It would therefore be absurd to continue to labour under the apprehension that the liberal intellectual approach to the current politics of security constitutes anything close to a critical intervention contesting the current regime in any form. A critique of liberalism should not be surprised by the erection of a facade to mask the reality of liberal politics but we should note the specific tool(s) used here to give the impression of a security regime that can, and does, withstand critique. Ultimately, the fact that liberal critiques are formulated giving so central a place to the language of (human) rights serves to set the parameters for all subsequent critique. Failing to circumscribe one's critique in the language of rights leads to rejection from any debate around security – legitimacy is ultimately the reserve of the human rights advocate. A critique that seeks to contest, or indeed name, the politics of security and the politics of human rights (as indeed they cannot be separated) is rendered literally to the extremes. The impenetrability of the politics of human rights lies in their status as an antipolitics[38] that complements, and indeed cannot be separated from, the politics of security that is in the same sense defined by the suppression of political action.

Rejecting security, rejecting human rights: affirming an alternative politics

The central function human rights play in legitimating the 'war on terror' is emblematic of the pivotal role they play in securing a monopoly of legitimacy for liberalism. If as Brown has noted, an analysis of this type is initially confronted by "the impossibility of saying anything generic about the political value of rights"[39] it is crucial that her subsequent conclusion be noted:

> It makes little sense to argue for them (rights) or against them separately from an analysis of the historical conditions, social powers, and political discourses with which they converge or which they interdict.[40]

In the context of the politics of security – within which human rights undoubtedly converge with the dominant political discourse – it is possible, and indeed necessary, to articulate a scathing critique and a wholesale rejection of human rights as tools for critique.

Furthermore, if as Brown notes human rights activism "displaces, competes with, refuses, or rejects other political projects"[41] this raises fundamental questions about the utility of human rights as a tool for political projects that seek to contest the politics of security. Indeed for any political project that seeks to abandon the constraints of liberal reformism and seeks instead to confront the world as the world is with a view to transform it, human rights reveal themselves to be not only of little utility but arguably a detrimental accompaniment. If a drive for collective justice – or indeed any true sense of justice which by definition must be collective – is to be at the core of emancipatory politics then human rights cannot, by way of their equation with liberal individualism, assist such a project. This revelation should provide real cause for concern for those on the left who seek to articulate critiques of the violence of liberal politics – including the current security politics – in the language of human rights.

So what then for an effective critique of security that refuses to be constrained by the language of human rights? If legitimacy is restricted to those interventions that refuse to contest the logic of security then a truly alternative politics will, within the current debate, be by definition illegitimate – accommodation within the current debate would be the mark of an insubstantial critique. Escaping the logic of security requires politicising security, naming it for what it is – the supreme concept of bourgeois society. We must abandon any notion that the current security regime in any sense constitutes an aberration from liberal principles and confronting the liberal intellectual is crucial in this task.

The central goal has to be one of politicisation and an outright opposition to any form of securitisation. This will lead to a polemical reaction from the security intelligentsia (and the liberal intellectual community) but confrontation with the logic of security must involve, if not begin with, confrontation with the intellectuals that provide it with a crucial source of legitimacy and render it closed to critique. If conflicts are marginalised through the discourse of security (and human rights) a truly political critique of security must (re)instigate these.

A truly alternative politics must ultimately be *against security*. It must refuse outright to work within the logic of security and eschew all validity of a reformist approach. The foundations of this project must be laid by an exposure of the current regime and a conscious process of cutting through the mystification that surrounds the politics of security. Exposing the depoliticisation that is at once a premise and consequence of the liberal intellectual's intervention and in turn seeking to oppose this through an explicit politicisation of the central issues of security and policing is the task of the *Anti-Security intellectual*. If we are to resist the concept of security altogether, as indeed we must from a perspective which refuses to grant the current status quo any legitimacy and seeks to transform it, then we must first acknowledge what security is and how it has historically emerged an almost impenetrable good.

Notes

1. Antonio Gramsci, *Selections from the Prison Notebooks* (London: Lawrence and Wishart Limited, 1971).
2. Mark Neocleous, *Critique of Security* (Montreal: McGill-Queen's University Press, 2008).
3. Peter Hallward, 'The Politics of Prescription', *South Atlantic Quarterly*, Vol. 104, No. 4, Fall 2005, pp. 769-789.
4. Carl Schmitt, *The Crisis of Parliamentary Democracy* (London: The MIT Press, 1988 [1923]); Mark Neocleous, 'Security, Liberty and the Myth of Balance: Towards a Critique of Security Politics', *Contemporary Political Theory*, Vol. 6, No. 2, 2007, pp. 131-149.
5. Richard Rorty, 'Fighting Terrorism with Democracy', in *The Nation*, October 21st, 2002, p. 3.
6. Michael Ignatieff, *The Lesser Evil: Political Ethics in an Age of Terror* (Edinburgh: Edinburgh University Press, 2005), p. 111.
7. Michael Walzer, *Arguing about War* (London: Yale University Press, 2004), p. 133.
8. This process involves a 'reduction of political motivations and causes to essentialized culture (where *culture* refers to an amorphous polyglot of ethnically marked religious and nonreligious beliefs and practices)' whose ultimate effect 'analytically vanquishes political economy, states, history, and international and transnational relations'. See, Wendy Brown, *Regulating Aversion: Tolerance in the Age of Identity and Empire* (Princeton: Princeton University Press 2008), p. 20.
9. Alongside the 'Culturalization of politics' these discourses of depoliticisation include: *Liberalism* (the legal and political formalism of liberalism); *Individualism*; *Market rationality*; and *Tolerance*, (Brown, *Regulating Aversion*).
10. The subject of human rights is for Badiou, split into active and passive beings and this split establishes a relationship within which the active subject takes on an intervening role to save or protect the passive victim that is utterly powerless ultimately as a result of its *subhumanity*. See, Alain Badiou, *Ethics: An Essay on the Understanding of Evil*, (London: Verso, 2001), pp. 9-13, [original emphasis].
11. Wendy Brown, '"The Most We Can Hope For......": Human Rights and the Politics of Fatalism', *The South Atlantic Quarterly*, Vol. 103, No. 2/3, Spring/Summer 2004, pp 453.

12. Michael Ignatieff, *Human Rights as Politics and Idolatry* (Princeton: Princeton University Press, 2001), pp. 173.
13. Badiou, *Ethics*, p. 13.
14. Ignatieff, 2005cited in Brown, *The Most We Can Hope For*, p. 454.
15. Ronald Dworkin, *Is Democracy Possible Here?: Principles for a new political debate* (Princeton: Princeton University Press 2006), p. 160.
16. This aspiration is the inline with the liberal aspiration *par excellence*: to overcome conflict and thus to overcome politics leaving only economic competition and the competition of opinions.
17. Richard Rorty, 'Human Rights, Rationality and Sentimentality', in Obrad Savic [Ed], *The Politics of Human Rights*, (London: Verso, 1999).
18. Rorty, *Human Rights, Rationality and Sentimentality*, p. 75, (original emphasis).
19. Wendy Brown, *Politics out of History*, (Princeton: Princeton University Press, 2001), p. 30.
20. In work done elsewhere I have devoted space to an analysis of state security policy and also to a fuller exposition of the position of the liberal intellectual. From this perspective I have been able to map more comprehensively the amazing convergence between the liberal intellectual and the liberal state in relation to security politics. See, Will Jackson, *The Politics of Liberty and Security: The new human rights approach and its role in the era of the 'war on terror'* (University of Salford, [PhD thesis], forthcoming).
21. Sarah Sewall, 'Introduction to the University of Chicago Press edition: A Radical Field Manual', United States Army and United States Marine Corps, *The U.S. Army/Marine Corps Counterinsurgency Field Manual*, (Chicago: University of Chicago Press, 2007), p. xxii.
22. Mark Neocleous, 'War as peace, peace as pacification', in *Radical Philosophy*, Issue. 159, 2010, pp 8-17, (emphasis added).
23. Brown, '*The Most We Can Hope For…*', p. 457.
24. Peter Gabel, 'Book Review: Taking Rights Seriously', *Harvard Law Review*, Vol. 91, No. 1, 1977, pp. 302-315.
25. Christopher Cox, Molly Whalen and Alain Badiou, 'On Evil: An Interview with Alain Badiou', *Cabinet Magazine Online* [internet], Issue 5, Winter 2001/02 -http://www.cabinetmagazine.org/issues/5/alainbadiou.php accessed 10/08/10.

26 For further explanation see Norman Geras and Nick Cohen 'The Euston Manifesto', *The New Statesmen*, [internet], 17 April 2006, Available at: http://www.newstatesman.com/200604170006 [Accessed 2/8/10].
27 Richard Rorty, *Achieving Our Country: Leftist Thought in Twentieth-Century America* (London: Harvard University Press 1998), p. 42.
28 Nick Cohen, *What's Left: How Liberals Lost Their Way*, (London: Fourth Estate, 2007), p. 14.
29 Ignatieff, *Lesser Evil*, p. 99.
30 Alan Johnson, 'The New Authoritarian Marxism: A Terrorist Theory of the State', *Dissent Magazine Blog*, May 17th 2010, http://www.dissentmagazine.org/atw.php?id=122, [Accessed 2/1/11].
31 Slavoj Zizek, *The Ticklish Subject: The Absent Centre of Political Ontology*, (London: Verso, 1999), p. 353.
32 Neocleous, 'War as Peace, Peace as Pacification' p. 16.
33 Costas Douzinas, *Human Rights and Empire: The political philosophy of cosmopolitanism*, (Abingdon: Rouledge-Cavendish, 2007), p.102.
34 Douzinas, *Human Rights and Empire*, p. 108.
35 Neocleous, *Critique of Security*, p. 183.
36 Neocleous, *Critique of Security*, p. 183.
37 Karl Marx 'On the Jewish Question' (1843), in *Early Writings*, (Harmondsworth: Penguin, 1975). See also, Mark Neocleous, 'Security, Liberty and the Myth of Balance: Towards a Critique of Security Politics', *Contemporary Political Theory*, 2007, Vol. 6, No. 2, pp.131-149.
38 Brown, *'The Most We Can Hope For'*, p. 454.
39 Wendy Brown, *States of Injury*, (Princeton: Princeton University Press 1995), p. 98.
40 Brown, *States of Injury*, p. 98.
41 Brown, *'The Most We Can Hope For'* p. 453.

[8]
Security: Resistance

HEIDI_RIMKE

Much of the writing about 'security' in the social sciences represents the dominant perspective of the privileged, powerful and wealthy, those who possess the social, political, cultural and economic capital to preside over and steer the dominating institutions of neoliberal society. This taken-for-granted and institutionally rewarded approach might be described as 'mainstream,' 'normative,' 'orthodox,' 'positivist,' 'conventional,' 'official,' or 'bourgeois' security studies. It is the sort of 'popular' material characteristically presented by corporate news/entertainment media, mainstream activists and academics, police chiefs and police organizations, governmental officials, and the upper ranks of the military-industrial-academic complex. As I have argued elsewhere,[1] dominant discourses become naturalized and normalized through mass communication, mass commodification and widespread circulation, such that the popularized versions reflect, maintain, and reproduce dominant social, political and economic interests in popular culture and the academy alike. These security discourses are thus taken here as dominant governing modes of thought. The task of critical thought, in contrast, is to provide the grounds of an anti-security politics, one which disrupts the relations of ruling intrinsic to the conceptual practices of power[2] that exalt and reify security discourses. This chapter should be seen as confronting the normativization of policing and the fetishization of security that enjoys a virtually unchallenged supremacy today.[3]

To understand the class violence that is capitalism, the approach aims to de-secure what can now be seen as the securitization of security discourses by making present the absence of critiques of police and policing in late capitalist society, particularly in the context of mass protest and resistance. The absence of critique provides a looping effect that secures the hegemony of security. Theoretically then, this approach is probably best described as a non-hegemonic form of intellectual counter-conduct with the aim of destabilizing the increasing normativization of security that underpins official violence. It explicitly rejects the dominant doxa as necessary and inevitable, and therefore beyond reproach and resistibility.

To do so, the essay focuses on the social processes and dynamics of contemporary public policing in the context of securing elite summits such as that seen in June 2010 in Toronto, Canada. Too much attention in the literature has been spent on analyzing private policing at the expense of examining public policing[4]. Public police in Canada receive ever greater budget expenditures, reporting the sixth consecutive year of economic growth in Canada. According to Statistics Canada, there were 69,299 active police officers in Canada in 2010, an increase of almost 2,000 officers from 2009. As of 2010, the number and cost of public police was at its highest rate since 1981.[5] This increase in public funding for police feeds into and legitimizes the security discourse despite the declining official crime rate coupled with an aging population.

The extravagant billion dollar security feast of the Toronto 2010 G20 elite summit demonstrates the priority of capital to carnage public funds at the expense of urgent social needs. Police and dominant economic interests profit from exploiting and criminalizing organized political resistance under the banner of 'security'. Over a period of a few days, more than 1100 people where captured by police constituting the largest mass arrest and most profitable security stunt in Canadian history. Policing resistance in the name of 'security' is thus a financially lucrative business that should be understood as forming part of the wider prison-industrial complex[6] or crime-control industry.[7] The siphoning of public funds in the name of security, the 'blue drain'[8] phenomenon, entails massive transfers of public funds reflecting the opportunistic exploitation of public resources by the security industry. The increasing policing of capitalist society despite a steady decrease in crime rates should occupy a central place in social and political thought, especially given the rise in unemployment and the mechanisms by which more and more bodies become absorbed, disciplined and exploited by the state's security apparatus. Yet despite the significant economic and political implications of heightened policing and increasing security rhetoric in contemporary society, the Left has generally failed to understand the police concept and thus has lost sight of how to use it.[9] This is especially the case when it comes to making sense of the growing repression and criminalization of political resistance in the early twenty-first century.

Policing as pacification, anti-security as resistance

The concept of anti-security can be understood as a means of addressing, challenging and moving beyond the hegemony of security. Given that the concept of security depends upon the concept of insecurity for its knowability, the notion of anti-security moves beyond the binarism underpinning the pacification efforts of Official narratives. Understood as the most powerfully productive and repressive political trope of contemporary politics, the emphasis on security means that at some fundamental level the order of capital is an order of insecurity. It is through this politics of in/security that the current wave of state repression is structured and legitimated demonstrating first and foremost the dominant concern of securing the insecurity that results from capitalist accumulation and political power. As this volume sets out to show, critical theory requires the concepts of pacification and anti-security to make sense of the processes and practices through which bourgeois civility and obedience is constituted, maintained, reproduced, and resisted. Thus, if security *is* pacification, as Mark Neocleous argues, then anti-security *is* resistance.

Dominant actors and decision-makers rely on audience assumptions and beliefs about danger, risk, and fear to achieve certain goals such as the suppression of social, political and economic dissent.[10] Since the nineteenth-century, if not before, the so-called 'dangerous class' provided the historical rationale for a style of governance that required enemies who were produced as the scourge threatening the purity of Western 'civilization' thereby fortifying the violent dividing practices upon which force relations of biopower depend.[11] Indeed, the history of the police as a security fetish is a history of "fear of the radical other".[12] As many have shown, the political economics of the security complex profit from the very enemies Officials and their experts claim to combat and from which they claim to 'protect' us.

Official campaigns of terror mobilize and capitalize on fear, resentment and anger. Governance through uncertainty, suspicion, and risk (re)produces a form of normativized citizenship while simultaneously encouraging the imaginary identification of threatening or disorderly Others, thereby justifying huge expenditures on "spectacular security"[13] that always already operate by way of spectacular insecurities. This can be witnessed in the one billion tax dollars spent on one weekend of elite security coupled with the spectacular insecurity of activists exercising their so-called constitutional rights to assemble and protest. The mass-mediated criminalization of the recent anti-G20 resistance in Toronto thus relied on the spectacle of the screen by communicating both spectacular security (for authorities, police and security agents, corporate elite, political leaders) and spectacular insecurity for protestors (and, indeed, anyone who just happened to be passing by). It is thus interesting to note that the authorities chose the former Toronto Movie Studio as the location to 'stage' and construct the make-shift G20 prison-house[14] (now referred to as 'Torontonamo') to detain arrestees over the weekend.

So too can the spectacular insecurity of capital be seen in the mass-mediated representations used to criminalize resistance as 'dangerous' while the dangers of security are masked and repackaged to placate the population in the name of law and order. Mass-mediated crime images and discourses hinge upon some version of the subhuman or inhuman subject. In the current context, this form of popular dehumanization can be seen in negative language (thugs, professional agitators, troublemakers, criminals) used to justify and rationalize police violence at mass protests including the on-going targeting of key anti-capitalist organizers in various communities across the country. It also draws attention to the significance of wider social policing of the Other, contributing to what Foucault refers to as the mentality to govern and be governed as normative and good, those forms of governance that 'free' and 'normal' individual subjects 'naturally' choose to undertake.

The historical and contemporary trend to present political activists as 'a permanent threat' provides the rationale for repressing and punishing dissent, as witnessed by the increased criminalization of resistance through 'new' and 'old' legal mechanisms. Given the class war that lies at the heart of collective resistance to capitalism, it is fitting that G20 police secured their divine right to 'suspend' all civil rights by taking political prisoners under the World War II law, the 1939 Public Works Protection Act. The impromptu invention of the 'five-metre rule' permitted police the power to ID, search and/or arrest anyone within five meters of the security fence, an arrangement that was secretly rubber-stamped by Liberal Premier Dalton McGuinty's cabinet at the request of the Toronto Police Chief. Authorities thus purposefully used their legal power to essentially enforce a law that did not exist given that 'by law' police could exercise those broad security powers only inside the fence.[15]

Demonization can be clearly seen with relation to dominant media portrayals of anarchism, particularly when Conservative Cabinet Minister Stockwell Day promised a 'security crackdown' on anarchists who were also blamed for travel disruption.[16] Through spectacular imagery, fear mongering and police-led disinformation campaigns reported uncritically in the mainstream media, the public are encouraged to side with the state and the police and against activists. It is the effects of so-called advanced capitalism, after all, that form the roots of domination and thus resistance. Fear, anger, resentment, repulsion, and anxiety are incited and promoted by mainstream spectacular visual images, such as those broadcasting a 'Top 10 Most Wanted' poster for anti-G20 activists or purposefully allowing police cars to burn on the streets for hours to provide media opportunities. Such mass-mediated spectacularization of resistance is necessary for Official narratives of 'dangerous strangers' or 'outsiders' attending summit protests. Spectacular criminalization not only operates to justify mass police domination and violence, it also incites everyday subjects to engage in policing practices. The point of activism is to unseat the permanence of domination by engaging in permanent resistance, whether that occurs on the streets, on campuses, or in communities, workplaces or public buildings. The challenge to capital spurs on multiple actions and strategies of resistance to the domination and exploitation at the heart of capitalist societies. As upholders of the status quo, police are key reproducers of this order.[17]

Rather than view insecurity as an historical effect of capitalist social relations of production and consumption, security discourses deflect attention from the very social, political and economic order that create individual and collective uncertainties. In the case of the G20, they transposed disorder onto activists in attempts to fabricate a restored social order through police power and the rhetoric of law and order. Thus, the promotion of crime, deviance and disorder legitimates Official policies, actions and mandates even when they are viewed as violating constitutional and civil rights. It is only by shaping insecurity that security attempts to secure.[18] Insecurity is thus socially necessary to the organizing and ordering of fears and anxieties that so-called civil(ized) modern neoliberal subjects - socialized through the conflation of propriety and property - are *expected and incited* to experience.[19] Despite popular discourses and misrepresentation of political disobedience, organized resistance to the capitalist order is our collective strength, not our problem.

> Our problem is civil obedience. Our problem is the numbers of people all over the world who have obeyed the dictates of the leaders of their government and have gone to war, and millions have been killed because of this obedience. Our problem is that people are obedient all over the world in the face of poverty and starvation and stupidity, and war, and cruelty. Our problem is that people are obedient while the jails are full of petty thieves and all the while the grand thieves are running the country. That's our problem.[20]

The fetishization of property and propriety, arguably the cornerstone of policing-oriented bourgeois subjectivities, must therefore remain central to critical analyses of capital and its security regime. The moralizing sadism of bourgeois subjectivities that treat property as a victim and state victims as collateral damage for securing property is a product of the neoliberal governmental rationalities constituting the bourgeois individualism characterizing the capitalist order. Thus, crimes against property, not state violence against people, remain at the heart of the law in bourgeois society.[21] The property/propriety dualism can also be seen in the bourgeoisification of activism in contemporary political movements that side with the police rather than the criminalized though either silence or active demonization. The bourgeoisification is particularly evident in authoritarian tendencies to conflate property destruction with 'violence' and fails to understand even a rudimentary liberal legal definition of violence. Although many deaths result from the social cannibalism necessary to the violent practices of capitalism,[22] until more recently, police have rarely been the target of the kind of public rage (and fear) that have been directed against the Other.

The rule of law is usually seen as the hallmark of what is popularly referred to as 'liberal democracy'. Legal processes and principles such as constitutionalism, equality of all before the law and judicial review are taken to be integral parts of modern neoliberal democracy; a civilized society that protects the liberty and security of the person. The rule of law is especially key in understanding the dominant assumptions about democracy and thus has become inseparable from other democratic principles such as civil liberties, consensual governance and political accountability.[23] Neoliberal debates over 'rights' obscure the underlying historical struggles over power, privilege, and property aimed at controlling identities, bodies, land and resources.[24] Pacification thus occurs through the myth of 'democratic policing' by giving the appearance of justice via the rule of law while veiling Official practices of violence and injustice in all spheres of human life.

The dominant security doxa reifies the liberal fairy-tale of democratic policing and thus does not view the absence of police as liberatory but rather as dangerous. As Neocleous has argued, following Marx, "security *is* the concept of the police...Security is part of the rationale for social order…it is under the banner of 'security' that police often marches".[25] Statism and liberal legalism operate in tandem to secure illusions of due process, constitutional rights, and the rule of law. The 'statist political imaginary' employs a certain mode of thought and a distinct form of vocabulary shared by individuals with very different positions and politics and is so ubiquitous that it has assisted the state in setting the limits on the theoretical imagination. The aim of critique, in contrast, is to imagine the end of the state (and thus an end to the possibility of fascism).[26] The anarchist slogan, 'kill the cop in your head' speaks to, and directly challenges, the micro-fascism embodied in generalized policing practices that everyone is expected to enact and exhibit. As Foucault once wrote: "The strategic adversary is fascism…the fascism in us all, in our heads and in our everyday behavior, the fascism that causes us to love power, to desire the very thing that dominates and exploits us".[27]

The criminalization of resistance should be understood as a permanent feature of the security doxa defining the social and political landscape since at least the early 2000's. The wide police sweep in Toronto elicited a response from the Canadian Civil Liberties Union (CCLA) in cooperation with the National Union of Public and General Employees (NUPGE). The collective shock of what should be seen as routine police conduct - state violence that anarchists and the poor, for example, have always experienced - produced investigative reports based on public hearings. Any formal inquiry is thus likely due to the fact that some of those arrested included various 'respectable citizens' such as members of mainstream media, human rights observers, lawyers, and passersby who were scooped up off the streets rather than the usual 'rabble' of striking workers, indigenous warriors, homeless and anarchist activists. Further, the liberal fantasy that a formal public inquiry will effect systemic, meaningful change fails to understand that the primary purpose of official enquiries is to placate the population by relegitimating political authority through the symbolic appearance of accountability and justice.

The House of Commons Standing Committee on Public Safety and National Security also released a scathing report calling for a full public inquiry into G20 police misconduct that included beatings, unjustified mass arrests, racist, sexist, and homophobic taunts, inhumane prison conditions, and refusal of access to legal representation and legal counsel.[28] Others contend that they experienced threats of rape from their police captors,[29] a centuries-old weapon of war, just as weapons of sexual violence have been tools for patriarchal and colonial domination.

The Canadian Civil Liberties Association and the National Union of Public and General Employees released their report in February 2011 based on three days of public hearings held in November 2010. The report notes that "security efforts... failed to come up to the standard of constitutional commitments". According to the findings, "police conduct and actions were at times disproportionate, arbitrary and excessive". This finding was confirmed by several witnesses who stated that "a concerted effort by police to terrorize participants...While in detention, some demonstrators experienced strip-searches, insults and discriminatory comments, and were held for more than 57 hours. Some said that they were handcuffed for more than 15 hours, and were deprived of food or water for more than eight hours. A number of detainees were also denied the right to speak to a lawyer. The Committee was also told that a number of witnesses were denied access to their essential medication, including insulin and anti-depressants".[30]

According to the Conservative Members of this Committee, however, "rather than focussing on the important issues of security, the Opposition Coalition focussed on impugning the good work done by Canadian law enforcement officers", and claimed that the summit was an "unmitigated success": "The irresponsible and inaccurate recommendations contained within this report are ... merely an attempt by the Opposition Coalition to score political points at the expense of Canadian law enforcement officers". While overt state repression against anti-capitalist resistance is part and parcel of capitalist order, the number of arrested and detained that weekend has set an ominous new precedent for the governmental legitimation and rationalization of unlimited police powers. Furthermore numerous key anarchist organizers and activists have become political prisoners of the capitalist state through both custodial and non-custodial settings. The Toronto G20 also provided the ideal social laboratory to test the general response to police repression of resistance movements.

The continual redeployment of security resources both domestically and internationally against subversive groups can be described as the effect of the on-going war against any or all disobedient and defiant subjects. Only the state, through its rhetoric of asserting its ability to act for the common good, is capable of sustaining, maintaining, and increasing class conflict and class domination in attempts to not only absorb but to profit from the inevitabilities of resistance capitalism has produced. Thus, to demand security - and therefore increased policing - is inevitably a demand for greater state repression in the service of wealth and privilege by expanding 'discretionary' (and discriminatory) police power.[31]

Dangerous anarchy

Regardless of the extent to which one thinks the revival of anarchism since the late 90s is in fact a real trend,[32] the 'spectre of anarchism' haunting present capitalist society is certainly central to the promotion of 'law and order' and the political domination of the social field. Blaming something called 'anarchism' for practices of state violence in the form of mass police brutalization is part of the authoritarian logic that runs through security discourse. Such uncritical thinking and speaking has become part of the bourgeoisification of Western activism, in which those promoting 'peaceful' civil obedience at some level identify with the bourgeoisie by choosing to side with the state and police. Referring to the police as 'our cops'[33] is symptomatic of this very problem.

For those seeking to challenge the hegemony of security, the state with its vast and complex array of laws, prisons, courts, police and armies stands not as the defender of social justice against inequality but as a primary cause of injustice and oppression.[34] Proudhon's quote from 1851 highlights the violent practices of government:

> To be governed is to be kept in sight, inspected, spied upon, directed, law-driven, numbered, regulated, enrolled, indoctrinated, preached at, controlled, checked, estimated, valued, censured, commanded, by creatures who have neither the right nor the wisdom nor the virtue to do so. To be governed is to be at every operation, at every transaction noted, registered, counted, taxed, stamped, measured, numbered, assessed, licensed, authorized, admonished, prevented, forbidden, reformed, corrected, punished. It is, under pretext of public utility, and in the name of the general interest, to be placed under contribution, drilled, fleeced, exploited, monopolized, extorted from, squeezed, hoaxed, robbed; then, at the slightest resistance, the first word of complaint, to be repressed, fined, vilified, harassed, hunted down, abused, clubbed, disarmed, bound, choked, imprisoned, judged, condemned, shot, deported, sacrificed, sold, betrayed; and to crown all, mocked, ridiculed, derided, outraged, dishonoured. That is government; that is its justice; that is its morality.[35]

However, as Bourdieu and Wacquant add, the

> violence of the state…is not exercised solely (or even mainly) upon the subaltern, the mad,

the sick, and the criminal. It bares upon us all in a myriad minute and invisible ways, every time we perceive and construct the social world through categories instilled in us via our education. The state is not only 'out there', in the form of bureaucracies, authorities and ceremonies. It is also 'in here', ineffaceably engraved within us, lodged in the intimacy of our being in the shared manners in which we feel, think and judge.[36]

Demanding arrest and criminalization of the 'baddies'[37] by condemning activists rather than police violence contributes to the reproduction of class domination. The fetish for the 'peaceful protestor' should thus be understood as a technique of pacification that conceals and fortifies the class violence of capitalism. It also secures social, political and economic domination by effectively barring the solidarity and support necessary to winning the class war. Such historical amnesia and political myopia ultimately plays into the hands of the State and its security agenda by maintaining or increasing dividing practices. While such tactics are certainly not new, such practices need to be called out, especially when pleas for criminalization are coming from self-professed Leftists themselves. Formal and informal targeting of an entity called 'anarchism' is thus more than an issue of 'public order'; it is a clear example of suppressing resistance to the benefit of economic and political elites.

The historical record on police infiltration, agent provocateurs, and false flag operations, such as the black bloc provocateurs wearing police boots who were exposed at the 'Security and Prosperity Partnership' meeting of elites in Montebello, Quebec 2007, should act as a reminder of the complications involved in taking the dominant representations and narratives at face-value. Furthermore, the numerous 'black-clad' activists at the Toronto G20 who sported various kinds of neon markers on knapsacks, and brightly coloured socks or shoelaces should alone raise questions about anarchist authenticity. Evidence of G20 police posing as 'anarchists' is duly documented by numerous videos showing so-called black-bloc anarchists scurrying behind police lines, and offers more than a little hint at the fact that police infiltration and imitation of black block anarchists sought to discredit the protests. Enough evidence has surfaced to indicate that the police will and do infiltrate radical organizations with the aim of destabilizing resistance by sowing suspicion and innuendo to instil insecurities in the wider movement. The 'whodunnit?' game is thus probably best left to the police and bureaucrats as militants have nothing to gain by playing cop profiler except to acknowledge and understand that it is a normative police tactic which is why most militant activists increasingly organize as autonomous affinity groups and communicate knowledge and information on a 'need-to-know' basis.[38]

The police require socially choreographed spectacles to produce and reproduce the fear and anger that can then be recuperated and reconfigured as evidence to justify the apparatuses and practices of securitization. The effects of emotional practices of power and security contribute to increased policing and repression of undesirables or troublemakers.

Organized resistance, whether in the form of labour strikes, street protests, occupations or blockades will continue to be represented as criminally dangerous thus serving the expansionary logic of the security regime. Elite summits provide the theatre of security an ideal stage to flex the strong arm of the state. Those represented as 'enemies' in the mantra of law and order help the state legitimize political manoeuvres such as kettling, invention of laws, weapons and technologies of crowd control, witch-hunts, assault, infiltration and covert surveillance.

The myth of domestic and international 'peacekeeping' is based upon Official security narratives that rest upon a glorified notion of the benevolent, paternal state that exists to protect and ensure the security of its citizens – a paramount assumption used to legitimate the state's existence. Governments thus resort to spectacular security with broad arrest powers in the face of resistance from below, lest the state is literally viewed as weak in its capacity to discipline the dangerous Other. In capitalism, the 'security of the people' and 'the security of the capital' are diametrically opposed yet become re-aligned through neoliberal discourses and myths that conflate and are eventually sublated under 'the security of capital'. A major provision of security discourses, practises and technologies is thus geared towards not only deflecting attention from root causes of class domination, inequalities and conflict but, equally significantly, to placate or pacify the population. By reproducing the very divisions and categories upon which the biopolitics of the criminal sciences has been based, the problematic of crime appears to be objectively resolved when in fact such constructions can be said to be the most powerful exercise of state power of all – the power to define, delineate and control criminality.

Modern insecurity and security are mutually constitutive, thus signaling the necessity of theorizing both in relation to one another, as well as the manner(s) in which this dualism is maintained through the political technologies of police. Policing of public protest reifies the highly controlled and restrictive processes of parliamentary democracy as the preferred form of political engagement and expression. Alternative forms of politics that challenge the pacifying politics of parliamentarianism are thus represented through the dominant security doxa as irrelevant, absurd, pathological or even criminal.

Spectacular insecurities are evoked by official discourses to justify the violence of poverty, occupation, war, and torture endemic to the capitalist world. Whether viewed historically or in the light of growing opposition and capitalist crisis, it is becoming more and more clear that pacification is thus class war exercised by other means.[39] By containing opposition, penalizing dissent, and repressing or erasing meaningful political debate, the criminalization of resistance operates under the guise of 'national security.' Slavish obedience to the security doxa contributes to marginalization, targeting entire communities, creating dangerous Others, and throttling resistance, with the latter intended to not only drive resistance under but also to provide a clear moral example and resounding legal lesson of the fate awaiting anyone who resists the status quo. Because resistance from below is a permanent threat to capital, the state will always move to quell, quash and punish those challenging or confronting its power. The resurgent intensification of state repression against activism and 'anarchism' since the end of the twentieth century is legitimated by a society that has now been almost completely colonized by the discourse of security.

Conclusion

The idea of security as a public good or part of a social contract between the state and its citizen-subjects - that is, the central assumption in all security discourse - never addresses situations and events where one party to the contract systematically fails to meet its obligations, as, for example, when the state purposely misleads, exploits, and harms its citizens. It also rests on one of the most ideological notions of all: that it is within the capacity of the police to serve and protect. It thus deliberately underestimates the capacity of policing to operate as the repository of public danger. "The rising wave of direct actions is not about defiance of law and order - rather it is a challenge that the regime of rule itself is illegitimate. Their order is not ours and the order they are tasked with keeping is not one we want kept (at demonstrations or otherwise)".[40] For those held captive by the pacifying neoliberal myths of our time, demanding last June that the G20 police do "their goddamned job," which is what, in fact, they were precisely doing.

At the very least, the documented G20 police conduct should cast radical doubt on the notion of police misconduct as nothing more than an aberration of a few 'rogue cops'. All evidence shows that police violence is not an issue of a few 'bad apples' but, rather, a key part of an apparatus designed for the social war of capital.

Radical scholarship from an anti-security perspective understands that activists that engage in symbolic and direct action to fight in solidarity with communities under attack face ongoing state repression in the form of collective criminalization. A new historical wave of campaigns of repression thus increasingly and brazenly punish and attempt to silence dissent in the name of 'security.' It has been suggested that the idea of striking a balance between security and liberty is a liberal myth that masks the fact that liberalism's key category is not liberty, but security,[41] and the mass criminalization of protest in Toronto demonstrates this precisely. But perhaps we might go further and argue that the ultimate target of security politics is freedom itself.

Notes

1. Heidi Rimke, 'Remembering the Sociological Imagination: Trans-disciplinarity, the Genealogical Method, and Epistemological Politics', *International Journal of Interdisciplinary Social Sciences*, Vol. 5, No. 1, 2010, pp. 239-254.
2. Dorothy Smith, *The Conceptual Practices of Power: A Feminist Sociology of Knowledge* (Toronto: University of Toronto Press, 1990).
3. Indeed, the 6 part *Toronto Star* investigative series published in October and November 2010 that probed the 7 million dollar a year Special Investigations Unit mandated to investigate police accused of injuring and killing civilians revealed little accountability on the part of the police. Yet the Star received such negative commentary on the newspaper's website that the paper was compelled to respond with an editorial defending investigative journalism. ('Are These Cops Above the Law?', *Toronto Star*, 28, 30, October 2010, and 1, 2, 3, 4, 5, November 2010).
4. Todd Gordon, 'The Political Economy of Law-And-Order Policies: Policing, Class Struggle, And Neoliberal Restructuring', *Studies in Political Economy*, Vol. 75, 2005, pp. 53-77, p. 74.
5. *Police Resources in Canada* (Ottawa: Canadian Centre for Justice Statistics, 2010), Catalogue no. 85-225-X, p. 7. Changes made to the Police Resources Report in May 2010 entailed removing figures on police operating expenditures in municipal police services as reported in previous years.
6. Angela Y. Davis, *Are Prisons Obsolete?* (New York: Seven Stories Press, 2003).
7. Nils Christie, *Crime Control as Industry: Towards Gulags, Modern Style* (London: Routledge, 2000).
8. B. Erickson, 'Good Networks and Good Jobs: The Value of Social Capital to Employers and Employees', in N. Lin *et. al.*, *Social Capital: Theory and Research* (New York: Aldine de Gruyter, 2001).
9. Mark Neocleous, *The Fabrication of Social Order: A Critical Theory of Police Power*. London: Pluto Press, 2000), p. 92.
10. David Altheide, 'Terrorism and the Politics of Fear', *Cultural Studies, Critical Methodologies*, Vol. 6, No. 4, 2006, pp. 415-439, p. 415.
11. Heidi Rimke, 'Constituting Transgressive Interiorities: C19th Psychiatric Readings of Morally Mad Bodies',' in A. Arturo (ed.), *Violence and the Body: Race, Gender and the State*. Indiana: Indiana University Press, 2003).

12 Neocleous, *Fabrication*, p. 61
13 Philip Boyle and Kevin D. Haggerty, 'Spectacular Security: Mega-Events and the Security Complex', *International Political Sociology*, Vol. 3, 2009, pp. 257–274.
14 "Film Studio Turned Police Centre", CBCnews.com, 21 June 2010, http://www.cbc.ca/canada/g20streetlevel/2010/06/g20-film-studio-turned-police-centre.html
15 Robert Ferguson, 'Province to Scrap Secret G20 Law', *Toronto Star*, 28 April 2011.
16 "Day Blames G20 Travel Alert on 'Small Group of Thugs'" CTV-Ottawa, 20 June 2010.
17 Neocleous, *Fabrication*, p. 65
18 Neocleous, *Fabrication*, p. 60
19 Heidi Rimke 'Consuming Fears: Neoliberal In/Securities, Cannibalization, and Psychopolitics', in Jeffrey Shantz (ed.), *Racism and Borders: Representation, Repression, Resistance*. (New York: Algora Publishing, 2010).
20 Howard Zinn cited in Earl Raab, *Major Social Problems* (New York: Harper & Row, 1973), p. 294.
21 Neocleous, *Fabrication*, p .76
22 Rimke, 'Consuming Fears', p. 10
23 Jennifer A. Widner, *Building the Rule of Law* (New York: W.W Norton, 2001).
24 Radha D'Souza 'The Rights Conundrum: Poverty of Philosophy Amidst Poverty', in R. Banakar (ed), *Rights in Context: Law and Justice in Late Modern Society* (Basingstoke: Ashgate, 2010); and, 'Liberal Theory, Human Rights and Water-Justice: Back to Square One?' *Law, Social Justice & Global Development Journal*, Vol. 1, 2008, pp.1-15.
25 Neocleous, *Fabrication*, p.44
26 Mark Neocleous, *Imagining the State* (Maidenhead: Open University Press, 2003), pp. 1, 3-6, 7.
27 Michel Foucault, 'Preface', in Gilles Deleuze and Felix Guattari, *Anti-Oedipus: Capitalism and Schizophrenia* (1972), trans. Robert Hurley, Mark Seem and Helen R. Lane (Minneapolis: University of Minnesota Press, 1983), p. xiii.
28 Issues Surrounding Security at the G8 and G20 Summits. Report of the Standing Committee on Public Safety and National Security, Federal Government of Canada, March 2011.

29 Daniel Libby, 'Interview with Amy Miller, Director of "Myths for Profit"', *Toronto Media Co-Op*, 1 January, 2011.
30 *G20 Toronto Breach of the Peace: A Citizen's Inquiry into Policing and Governance at the Toronto G20 Summit*, Canadian Civil Liberties Association Report, February, 2011.
31 Neocleous, *Fabrication*, p. 61.
32 Richard J. F. Day, *Gramsci is Dead: Anarchist Currents in the Newest Social Movements* (Toronto: Between the Lines/Pluto Press, 2005); Barbara Epstein, 'Anarchism and the Anti-Globalization Movement', *Monthly Review*, Vol. 53, No. 4, 2001, pp. 1-14; David Graeber, 'The New Anarchists', *New Left Review*, Vol. 13, Jan-Feb, 2002, pp. 61-73; Lynne Owens, 'Making the News: Anarchist Counter Public Relations on the World Wide Web', *Critical Media Studies* Vol. 20, No. 4, 2003, pp. 335-361; Jeffrey Shantz, *Active Anarchy: Political Practice in Contemporary Movements* (Lanham: Lexington Books, 2011); Gordon Uri, 'Anarchism Reloaded', *Journal of Political Ideologies*, Vol. 12, No. 1, 2007, pp. 29-48.
33 Naomi Klein, *Fences and Windows: Dispatches From the Front Lines of the Globalization Debate*, (Toronto: Vintage Canada, 2002). p. 128; 'Police and Tasers: Hooked on Shock' *NaomiKlein.com*, 2008; and on the 2010 Toronto G20 police specifically, see http://www.digitaljournal.com/article/293973.
34 Shantz, *Active Anarchy*, p. 22.
35 Pierre-Joseph Proudhon, *The General Idea of the Revolution in the 19th Century*, trans. John Beverley Robinson (New York: Dove, 2003), p. 294.
36 Pierre Bourdieu and Loic Wacquant, *The State Nobility: Elite Schools in the Field of Power*. (Cambridge: Polity Press, 1998), p. xviii.
37 Judy Rebick quoted in Sunny Freeman, 'Black Bloc Tactics Alarm Police', *Canadian Free Press*, 28 June 2010; also see "Statement by Ken Georgetti, President of the Canadian Labour Congress on Vandalism Surrounding Toronto G20 Meeting", 26 June 2010, http://www.canadianlabour.ca/national/news/statement-ken-georgetti-president-canadian-labour-congress-vandalism-surrounding-toron
38 For example, black bloc organizing often entails closed meetings, where location is revealed last minute by telephone, and to

gain entry each participant must be verified or vouched for by a minimum of two others present. Awareness of covert state tactics of infiltration and surveillance has thus resulted in an anarchist counter-security security culture.

39 Mark Neocleous, 'War as Peace, Peace as Pacification', *Radical Philosophy*, Jan-Feb, 2010, pp. 8-17.
40 Jeffrey Shantz 'They Were Doing Their G-D Job: On Policing Protest', 3 July 2010, http://jeffshantz.ca/node/17
41 Mark Neocleous, 'Security, Liberty and the Myth of Balance: Towards A Critique of Security Politics', *Contemporary Political Theory*, Vol. 6, 2007, pp. 131-149.

[8]
Security and the Void: Aleatory Materialism contra Governmentality

RONJON_PAUL_DATTA

'What are we, are we superfluous in this age when what should be happening is not happening?'[1]

Introduction: Nothing Really Matters

In *Anti-Security: A Declaration*, Mark Neocleous and George Rigakos state that it is necessary to "fight for an alternative political language that takes us beyond the narrow horizon of bourgeois security and its police powers". My aim in this piece is to provide some initial reflections and formulations about how aleatory materialism may be of use in doing so.[2] I argue that aleatory materialist theorizing about the discursive and subjective constitution of an existential orientation to *what isn't happening, but just might emerge* (in aleatory materialist terms, 'the void'; 'nothing') will be of help in generating this kind of 'alternative political language'. This is in contrast to what I will call 'security subjectification' that orients people to their own activities and plans and to those of others as well, in a precarious world, constituted through the various discourses and practices of securitization central to governing (whether through the use of private police, declaring martial law, fastening one's seat belt, or insuring collateralized debt obligations). I view securitization, in its broadest sense, as a concern with shaping what a group of people with some say and power over a social circumstance, don't want to have happen (i.e., 'emergencies' generated in the void), or minimally, or a concern with finding ways of mitigating the concentration of catastrophic money costs of the emergence of events that adversely effect people's plans (hence, for example, the preference for 'civil remedies' in resolving litigation). I contend that the hegemonic discourse of 'government' and 'development' constitutes subjects subjugated to what is deemed to be an 'improved' future that in turn depends on secured conditions in which the pursuit of development occurs.[3] In terms of this governmentality, contemporary social life is treated as having a void that requires 'a little extra life', a focus that serves as a key justification of police, at least in its facilitative form.[4] Crucially, police as practice about how to develop the potential of all facets of humans social activity, was deemed a means to 'supply the state with a little extra strength' and from that, make it more secure relative to competitor, potentially enemy states.[5] This suggests that we are more than governed through an imagined future, improved, state of affairs.[6] We are subjugated in the present by a concern for achieving this better future, leaving us blind to the naturalisations of the capricious dominations and violence that come with security, amounting to an open war on the possible. This produces a form of discursive closure around possibilities for social organization and coordination.[7] Yet, to render security subjectification itself 'null and void' means confronting a different void, namely the void of a political task to be accomplished, even if deemed impossible, requiring a heterodox political metaphysic and existential orientation in which commitment to the goal of development (typically a commitment to the conditions of capital accumulation) is displaced in favour of thinking about unactualised conditions and potentials for differently problematising collective futures and fates.

Admittedly, what I do is abstract metatheorising and I have sacrificed discussion of case-study diagnostics, especially as concerns political crimes, for the sake length.[8] But, I do hope that the provisional theorems presented below provide some basis for further work.

Elements of Aleatory Materialism: Chance Encounters and the Void

Aleatory materialism, as developed by Louis Althusser, is a materialism of chance encounters committed to taking contingency seriously and following through with the theoretical and practical/political consequences.[9] Aleatory materialism fundamentally rejects all teleologies about history, politics and social life and sees teleological reasoning as the definitive feature of ideology.[10] In elaborating an aleatory materialism, Althusser sought to explicate a theoretically plausible materialist concept of the conditions of a politics that effectively de- and re-structures a social formation, creating a new social formation. Epicurus' atomism, Machiavelli's *The Prince* and Marx's discussion of original accumulation in *Capital*, serve as major reference points. Each of these three figures offer elements pertinent to thinking differently about security.

For Epicurus, a world comes into being when atoms falling in a void (i.e., elements that have no relation or contact with each other) have a chance encounter. Both the atoms and the void in which they fall are real. It is a minute swerve - the clinamen - in the trajectory of an atom falling in the void that is originary of a world, but without this being determined by an underlying, previously posited reason or a *telos* - it just happens. The swerve of an atom leads to an encounter between one atom and the one next to it, "and from encounter to encounter, a pile-up and the birth of a world - that is to say, of the agglomeration of atoms induced, in a chain reaction, by the initial swerve and encounter"[11]. For Althusser, "the world may be called *the accomplished fact* in which, once the fact has been accomplished, is established the reign of Reason, Meaning, Necessity and End. But *the accomplishment of the fact* is just a pure effect of contingency, since it depends on the aleatory encounter of atoms due to the swerve of the clinamen. Before the accomplishment of the fact, before the world, there is only *the non-accomplishment of the fact*".[12] A contingent combination of elements thus makes it possible for there to be a world that lasts in which making plans becomes possible.

Drawing on Machiavelli, Althusser stresses that politics and history happen when there is a chance or contingent encounter between virtue and fortune, i.e., a virtuous political agent (a new prince or politician) and a conjuncture favourable to the political project of a new prince to found a new kind of political and social order.[13] If the encounter between virtue and fortune lasts, then it will have accomplished the 'impossible'.[14] Politicians concerned with the new, deemed impossible in terms of the dominant discursive coordinates of a situation, occupy a non-place (void) in a conjuncture: they really don't belong since they don't play the part of a subject doing something that would contribute to the reproduction of an existing state of affairs. Crucially, social formations are underdetermined by the exceptional quality of politics in relation to a state of rule.[15] Underdetermination means the circumstance that the potentials within a social formation are not exhausted by the actually existing arrangement of social forces. So, the atomistic conception of the aleatory constitution of a world from which then emerges properties like ends, reason, etc., gives us conceivable futures. Machiavelli then gives us a way to think about how to undermine those futures by transforming their material conditions of existence, i.e., rearranging elements of a world to constitute *another world* by introducing the voiding powers of politics to dissolve the bonds that combine elements as elements of a world. The *void* of politics is thus suggestive of an *anti-security*, since aiming to void the conditions of stability and order required for imposing plans about the future and aiming to secure their realisation.

Althusser also emphasizes the extent to which a materialism of contingency is central to Marx's account of the emergence of capitalism, if one attends to the discussion of "original accumulation" in *Capital*.[16] For Althusser, it is the chance encounter that endures between the masses displaced by the use of force and violence from lands they were once able to use in common as part of producing their means of subsistence, and entrepreneurs with capital, that transforms both into productive forces under the social relation between wage-labour and capital thus to form the basis of the capitalist mode of production. Original accumulation provides Althusser a way of thinking about how the atoms of former peasants in the void (as evinced by massive migrations to urban centres) displaced by violence, played a role in securing the conditions for capitalist social relations of production, exploitation and capital accumulation.

Crucially, aleatory materialism places a great deal of emphasis on the emergence of the new from the absence/void of its ostensible, actual requisite conditions. I take emergence as central because the concept indicates the importance of the socio-historically contingent formation of new kinds of social forces irreducible to the causal powers of prior existing components such that when they are related in an enduring way, they generate new properties from the prior, contingently combined elements. At the same time, the newly formed enduring combinatory with its new properties affects the powers of the elementary components in a necessary and asymmetrical way, i.e., a hierarchy of determinations for the combinatory emerges that must be reproduced for the new powers of the combination to both exist *in potentia* and as actualised.

Althusser's aleatory materialist Marxism also returns Marxism to its special conception of the political in which state violence is central. Althusser criticizes Gramsci (and by extension Poulantzas and Foucault) for the "aberrant thesis" that "everything is political"[17]. The way Althusser puts it, drawing on Marx and Lenin, is to stress that the state is an 'instrument' or 'bludgeon', "that the dominant class uses to perpetuate its class domination".[18] But what makes the state machine-apparatus run is the fuel of violence.[19] The point he stresses is the unique *constitutive power of state violence* in politicized class struggle and in this regard, state violence is outside of what usually counts as politics (e.g., parliaments; partisan politics; op-ed pieces). Moreover, to be beholden to the notion that 'everything is political' is to cede the terrain of strategic, transformative political thought to a governmentalist problematic for which every action in every social institution is always already potentially a target of governmentalist developmentalism and hence the stuff of biopolitics.

The 1999 'Battle in Seattle' and similar struggles since perhaps serve as a necessary reminder for progressives that the state uses violence to suppress dissent, does so by right, and has extended the range of circumstances under which it can do so through anti-terrorism and emergency measures statutes. That anti-capitalist globalisation protestors around the world have been subjected to the violent suppression of dissent well highlights that the state is no paper tiger: the mundane, boring, administrative side of government is inseparable from the use of violence. To take one case in point, in Canadian law, manifestly the same actions and intentions are doubly inscribed, one in the register of the sovereign in the Criminal Code (e.g., public order offences including treason, sedition, insurrection and riots), and the other in the register of *security*, i.e., in terms of terrorism and emergency. In Canada's *Anti-Terrorism Act* the object of concern is very much 'security' and 'risk', very broadly understood. 'Terrorism' refers to:

> (b) an act or omission, in or outside Canada,
> (i) that is committed (A) in whole or in part for a political, religious or ideological purpose, objective or cause, and (B) in whole or in part

with the intention of intimidating the public, or a segment of the public, with regard to its security, including its economic security, or compelling a person, a government or a domestic or an international organization to do or to refrain from doing any act, whether the public or the person, government or organization is inside or outside Canada, and (ii) that intentionally(A) causes death or serious bodily harm to a person by the use of violence, (B) endangers a person's life, (C) causes a serious risk to the health or safety of the public or any segment of the public, (D) causes substantial property damage, whether to public or private property, if causing such damage is likely to result in the conduct or harm referred to in any of clauses (A) to (C), or (E) causes serious interference with or serious disruption of an essential service, facility or system, whether public or private, other than as a result of advocacy, protest, dissent or stoppage of work that is not intended to result in the conduct or harm referred to in any of clauses (A) to (C) (Section 83.01).[20]

Because of this, legal scholar Kent Roach argues that Canadian anti-terrorism laws and the Emergencies Act in effect criminalize politics.[21]

The thematics of contingency, original accumulation, the radical reconstitution of social formations, and the crucial linkage between the state and violence and make aleatory materialism pertinent to an analysis of security. But most importantly, aleatory materialism requires constantly thinking in terms of politics, political subjectivation,[22] the void and *a* future (a contingent one that could emerge). At the same time however, Foucault's approach to government with its valorization of security also shows that contingency and the future are of substantial concern to the activity of governing, not least in its liberal forms.[23] I now turn to these features of government.

Governmentality, Security and the Future

Foucault's analytics of power and government finds that the 'governmentalization of the state' has been decisive in modern politics.[24] He focuses his attention on the rationales and problems of a range of discourse concerned with the activity of government, for which he coins the term 'governmentality'. Governmentality is a system of political thought concerned with knowing what can be developed in the life of a population, attending to its individualized and totalized elements, within a secured territory, crucially, secured both internally from rebellion and immorality, and externally from other potentially bellicose states. State governing is an exercise of power involving finding out about, intervening in, and shaping what people are doing by facilitating some actions and placing obstacles to others. This is why Foucault formulates government as 'the conduct of conducts', 'action on an action' and that 'to govern, in this sense, is to structure the possible field of action of others'.[25] It is also preemptive,[26] targeting what the state does not want to have happen; heterodox futures are always in view.

The governmental concern with the future and development is derived from the pastoral sensibility of a concern with all and each, combined with leading toward the good. But, instead of a focus on salvation in the next world there emerges a concern for the "health, well-being and security of the people-flock as ensured by state apparatus or police".[27] Governmental development is exactly an intervention within a territory in order to "structure the possible field of action of others". The pastoral inflection in governmentality invents a notion of a government-shepherd that doesn't go anywhere; the measure is not movement, but temporal distributions of quantities within a jurisdiction (e.g., the rate of GDP growth). The government of states involves aligning and coordinating "a whole series of specific finalities that become the objective of government as such"[28]. This rationality introduces a historicity into political rule, a *telos*, inaugurating political modernity as a project of development and betterment. So, in contrast to previous concerns and aims of seeking to mirror the kingom of heaven and state of justice guided by the hand of Providence characteristic of medieval-monarchal rule, government has a different set of aims centred on the population.[29] This is the point where pastors meet police. We find some 'sheep' in the emergence of the doctrine of reason of state and its combination with 'police science' as elaborated in cameralism, *Polizeiwissenshaft* and statistics. Police provides knowledge of the objects to be improved and directed by government, providing knowledge of the place and contents to be developed. Police is very much a unique epistemic apparatus.[30]

Security, as a fundamental concern of government, is about "the future-oriented management of risks".[31] This is not a utopianism of police *per se* but a kind of *Realpolitik* from within the state that attends to what is likely, and on that basis, what can be enhanced. This is why security "deals in series of possible and probable events; it evaluates through calculations of comparative costs; it prescribes... by the specification of an optimal mean within a tolerable bandwidth of variation".[32]

In *Society Must Be Defended*, Foucault formulates his analysis somewhat differently, contrasting a "disciplinary technology of the body" with *regulation*:

> a technology which brings together the mass effects characteristic of a population, which tries to control series of random events that can occur in a living mass, a technology which tries to predict the probability of those events (by modifying it, if necessary), or at least to compensate for their effects. This is a technology which aims to establish a sort of homeostasis, not by training individuals, but by achieving an overall equilibrium that protects the security of the whole from internal dangers.[33]

The function of security, and by extension regulation then, is to "assure the integrity of 'natural phenomena, economic processes of population' [Foucault] while affirming the vulnerability of such natural processes and the need for a well modulated intervention in relation to them".[34]

The ends of government involves the perpetuation, not of security alone, but of fields in which to engage in a project of making a better future. Foucault is quite clear about this for as he argues, "security, protection against accidents', are a 'series of "worldly" aims', and have a finality".[35] This temporal dimension gives security a dynamism distinct from the usual conservative conceptions of order.

With governmentality, the conception of 'territory' also comes to mean more than bordered space. It is instead viewed in terms of a domain of regulation involving legal techniques as means for facilitating the life of the population. Cast in terms of the liberal understanding of the technique of using law, "law serves to demarcate and secure the boundaries between distinct fields of regulation such that their relative autonomy within their specific fields is reinforced"[36]. What law does in the hands of liberalism is delimit a field of legalities. In short, regulation through law is construed as a *constitutive mode of security*. Since government involves the concern with structuring the field of possible actions of others, to say 'structuring', in as much as it actualises a field of possible, probable and actual actions, *is to say 'territory'*; hence, territory does not pre-exist its security formation: the structuring produces the effect of territory. The over-arching aim of apparatuses of security is with constituting the regulatory mechanism of a shared fate (i.e., a future construed in terms of probabilistic distributions of events produced by people's actions). The concern with security in governmentality is not then the protection of the population, but is about ensuring the integrity of regulatory mechanisms, as evinced by the Canadian statutes noted above.

The logic of Foucault's analyses suggest that apparatuses of security are designed to "structure the possible field of actions of others" – apparatuses of security are deployed as a means for making the conduct of conduct possible. But, this, much like 'reasonableness' as described in *The History of Madness*, is never a done deal; neither 'reason' nor liberal freedom exist in-themselves, but rather are the remainder what is left over after having excluded what dominant groups deem to be unreasonable or an unrealistic or undesirable future goals to be pursued.[37] *Laissez-faire* development is what happens after having excluded what is deemed a security risk or threat closely tied to attempting to control or mitigate against that which would make development more difficult. As Foucault puts it in his discussion of popular justice, potentially 'dangerous' classes, from the point of view of the bourgeois state must choose between employment, joining the army, the police, going to the colonies or going to jail, to which it would be pertinent to add, going for further education and training.[38]

Governmentality, with its valorization of a better future, is tied to a peculiar kind of teleology, one that is homologous in many ways with capitalism. It is peculiar because of its formalism and proceduralism. For instance, any plan or policy programme contains is metrics and benchmarks for performance, implicitly or explicitly. The key comparator is improvement over what existed previously at some point after a programme has been implemented. It matters less what the nuts and bolts of doing so are (e.g., annual or bi-annual audits; quarterly reports) but more that the past, present, and future are subjected to the same form of temporal measures and basic procedures of record-keeping and reportage (i.e., technologies of surveillance and police), and on-going evaluations. The substance of the *telos* of government is manifested in the practical form of programming and evaluation. People's future plans are made in a present and our actions oriented toward that goal (whether positive or negative) are in the present, subjugating people to that future. What stitches this all together, not as discrete events, but as events with political significance, is government. Governmentality as a discursive technology thus means the continuous subjection to temporal series each subordinated to the value of improvement. In aleatory materialist terms, security functions *ideologically* given this discursively formalist teleology (i.e., all the procedures designed for attempting progress toward a better future).

Security Fetishism[39]

To transpose Marx's phenomenology of capitalism conceptualised as commodity fetishism that opens *Capital, Volume 1* into a Foucauldian register, a governmentalized world is a world spontaneously perceived as heading somewhere that will affect one's ability to achieve some future state deemed desirable. The fetish here is this temporality itself, part and parcel of the metaphysic of political modernity. However, just as the world spontaneously appears as a world of commodities, discrete items exchangeable through the equivalence of money, to this corresponds the non-sensible, concrete unthought of the singularity of the British capitalist social formation under its conjuncture and with it, the formation of its historical precondition, i.e., the secret of original accumulation. We do not see that violence when at the grocery store, we only perceive its empirically abstracted structural effects (e.g., those tomatoes). Indeed, this world beyond appearances is apprehensible solely via the development of adequate concepts. But, this unthought returns when that appropriation of the means of subsistence (property) is threatened with political uprising. As Foucault puts it, "what capitalism is afraid of, rightly or wrongly, since 1789, since 1848, since 1870, is insurrection and riot: the guys who take to the streets with their knives and their guns, who are ready for a direct and violent action. The bourgeoisie was haunted by this vision and it wants to let the proletariat know this is no longer possible".[40] The daily functioning of markets and their vicissitudes in which commodities are bought and sold appears as peaceable and as having an emergent order and (fractal) logic because the constitutive violence of original accumulation is a constant but sublimated presence. From the point of view of securitized subjectification, the world as it appears to us, is a means to an end: the phenomenology of modern subjectivity is dominated by this kind of orientation to a future to be achieved or striven for. To put a Nietzschean twist on this, *the idol/ fetish of the future* makes us blind to the domination to which we are subjected by focusing on developing for the future. Moreover, this is why I quite disagree with Foucault that a focus on power and government is distinct from an analysis of 'states of domination' that refer to circumstances "in which the power relations, instead of being mobile, allowing various participants to adopt strategies modifying them, remain blocked, frozen. When an individual or social group succeeds in blocking a field of power relations, immobilizing them and preventing any reversibility of movement by economic, political or military means"[41]. A futurized world, and with it, mechanisms of securitization (insurance, hedging, the distribution of payments for adverse events, dilution of contradictions) is a 'state of domination' subtended by violence, capriciously actualised. Foucault misses a level at which the violence of domination, the violence of the ontology of ourselves as governed and governing occurs, namely a *violence against the void*.

Contemporary Post-Politics and Security

For Post-Marxists, contemporary political culture is fundamentally post-political in which what is deemed to count as politics is reduced to the ways and means of social administration reserved for expert deliberation, justified by a myopic focus on development.[42] Foucault's account of government provides a way of explaining the contingent emergence of post-politics. But, as concerns the finalities of contemporary governmentality, arguably, "the future has already taken place".[43] This is a future that today tends to mean attempts to secure what was deemed to have recently, thankfully, taken hold of Western civilization, namely the world as it was coming into fruition between the fall of the Berlin Wall that began at 2:30 AM November 10, 1989 to the morning of September 11, 2001. This was a world safe for capital and the free societies in which it operates, where governing through competitive marketisation, be it in the economy, state apparatus or civil society, purportedly allows for maximal individual freedom since fostering and rewarding initiative and responsibility, creating the dynamic, self-actualizing individuals that make for vibrant societies (i.e., neoliberalism). In as much as people accept that we live in liberal democratic societies, characterised by the dominance of the goal of capital accumulation and representative parliamentary democracy, where the predominant form of freedom is freedom of choice in the purchasing of consumer goods, it is unsurprising that anti-capitalist globalization protesters are vilified, since what they appear to be protesting is the freedom and democracy that makes space for their protest possible. They are, in Mary Douglas' formulation, exactly 'dirt', 'matter out of place', not where they should be, i.e., at work, at school, at home, at the gym, etc., from the point of view of post-politics.[44] This in turn, in classic tautological form, justifies mass arrests: protesters must have been doing *something* wrong or else the police wouldn't have arrested them; the police are taken to be 'right' *a priori*. Such logic is exactly the kind of teleology that Althusser sought to challenge with his aleatory materialism.

Post-politics though is premised on its own disavowed past violent, constitutive politics. This is why it is important to keep the 'post-' in mind: post-politics is the territory of policy/police opened up by a now previous politics, the repetition of which by any other political agent is forbidden in the name of security. For example, one might consider the liberal use of terror in the nineteenth century.[45] Or, one might consider the excluded and actively suppressed non-male, non-white, non-propertied persons from the voting franchise and political offices. Or, one could note that post-political expert administration means a constant war on politics, a war on the void, against possibilities and emergence, a war against any future, other than the one already decided upon.

However, governmentalist post-politics is only made more perverse by security failures, i.e., by what are deemed 'emergencies'. What interests me about this, from a broader socio-historical perspective, is how governmental ineptitude fuels contemporary populist anti-elitism and anti-government sentiment. In what I call 'the cunning of liberal reason', populist reactions against the post-politics of 'liberal, cosmopolitan elites' become manifest as the substantive 'truth' of liberalism (i.e., people looking after themselves), unwittingly producing the concrete effectiveness of 'elitist' post-political, liberal governance. Crucially, capitalism in part generates its dynamism by making social life precarious, holding the threats of layoffs and cuts to compensation packages over people's heads. Collective security ostensibly trickles up and out from how individuals deal with their own precarious circumstances. For example, as the consequences of Hurricane Katrina so poignantly illustrate, it isn't too serious if security apparatuses fail. Rather, from the point of view of the cunning of liberal reason, the disaster became an opportunity for civil society organisations to do their thing, to reinvigorate the moral life of the community and this is what police and (liberal) governmentality exactly aims to do. Narratives of this kind of resurgence of civil society and sense of mutual obligation do strike me as a return to myths of an Edenic moment founding the liberal social contract, after the violence and destruction, of course.

Conclusion

To contrast aleatory materialism and governmentality means attending to a void: the discursive action is about where nothing yet is happening but might. Not surprisingly, the aleatory materialist opposition to all teleology means voiding any hope in a messianic Proletariat that of necessity must emerge from the concrete contradictions of capitalist development. Governmentality offers the void of a biopolitical lack (e.g., 'underdevelopment'; 'productivity gaps') in the present geared toward the goal of a new and improved future to be realized by warring against the void of the emergence of that which might undermine the conditions for achievement. This is a peculiar feature of governmentalist virtue – it involves an extended political economy of trying to govern what isn't actually there, except in the order of security discourse. (Liberalism and its valorized discourses of security and mechanisms of securitization have science fiction as an obverse). There is also the void of the post-political impasse in which there appears to be no alternative to expert administration, representative, parliamentary democracy plus capitalism secured in the last instance by state violence. And last, there is the aleatory materialist void of genuine political problematisation about the on-going work of the contingent formation of collective futures and fates. This is why, to me, a striking effect of modern political metaphysics is the extent to which our existential orientation means living in a world surrounded by the thought about some or other void. It also seem to me that the choice over which void, construed in which discourse, will affect the contours of an appropriate political language for anti-security and the forms of subjectivity made possible by that choice.

Notes

1. Michel Foucault, 'Power and Sex' *Politics, Philosophy, Culture: interviews and other writings 1977-1984*, Lawrence Kritzman, ed., (New York: Routledge), p. 121.
2. Louis Althusser, *The Philosophy of the Encounter* (New York: Verso, 2006); Louis Althusser, *Machiavelli and Us* (New York: Verso, 1999); Michael Dillon. 'Governing through contingency: The Security of Biopolitical Governance', *Political Geography* Vol. 26, No. 1, 2006, pp. 41-47.
3. Michel Foucault, *Security, Territory, Population* (New York: Palgrave Macmillan, 2006); Danica Dupont and Frank Pearce, 'Foucault *contra* Foucault: Rereading the Governmentality Papers', *Theoretical Criminology*, Vol. 5, No. 2, 2001, pp. 123-158; Suzan Ilcan and Lynn Phillips, 'Developmentalities and Calculative Practices: The Millennium Development Goals', *Antipode*, Vol. 42, No. 4, 2010, pp. 874-844; Michael Dillon, 'The Security of Governance', *Global Governmentality*, in Wendy Larner and William Walters (eds.), (New York: Routledge, 2004), pp. 79-81.
4. Michel Foucault, 'Omnes et Singulatim', *The Essential Foucault*, eds. Paul Rabinow and Nikolas Rose (New York: The New Press, 2003), pp. 197.
5. Foucault, 'Omnes et Singulatim', p. 197.
6. For a compelling Foucauldian reconceptualisation of the relationship between the problematisation of the future ('futurity') and law, see Ben Golder and Peter Fitzpatrick, *Foucault's Law* (New York: Routledge, 2009). For them, 'any society or political formation, must, in order to continue in being, have some constituent regard to futurity. Such an attunement or orientation to futurity imports both an incorporative engagement with the future [...] but also an unconditional openess to what in the future remains irreducibly to come' p. 101.
7. Cf. Golder and Fitzpatrick's distillation of a dominant Foucauldian thesis about 'modernity as a time of closure, a denial of possibility and alterity', *Foucault's Law*, p. 103.
8. As concerns Foucault on revolutionary politics, political crimes like sedition, and justice, see his neglected, but incisive commentary in Michel Foucault, 'On Popular Justice: A Discussion with Maoists', in *Power/Knowledge*, ed. Colin Gordon (New York: Pantheon Books,

1980), pp. 1-36. For some pertinent literature that has informed my own reflections see: Barry Wright, 'Quiescent Leviathan? Citizenship and National Security Measures in Late Modernity', *Journal of Law and Society*, 1998, Vol. 25, No. 2, pp. 213-236; Frank E. Hagan, *Political Crime: Ideology and Criminality* (Boston: Allyn and Bacon, 1997); Jarret S. Lovell, *Crimes of Dissent* (New York: New York University Press, 2009); Kenneth McNaught, 'Political Trials and the Canadian Political Tradition', *The University of Toronto Law Journal*, 1974, Vol. 24, No. 2. pp. 149-169.

9 See in particular, Althusser, *Philosophy*; Althusser, *Machiavelli and Us*.
10 Louis Althusser, *Philosophy*, p. 190.
11 Louis Althusser, *Philosophy*, p. 169.
12 Althusser, *Philosophy*, pp. 168-9.
13 Althusser, *Machiavelli and Us*.
14 Althusser, *Machiavelli and Us*, pp. 52, 56.
15 Althusser, *Machiavelli and Us*, pp. 17-18; Francois Matheron, 'The Recurrance of the Void in Louis Althusser', *Rethinking Marxism*, 1998, Vol. 10, No. 3, p. 31.
16 Althusser, *Philosophy*, pp. 39-44.
17 Althusser, *Philosophy*, p. 150.
18 Althusser, *Philosophy*, p. 68.
19 Althusser, *Philosophy*, pp. 81-85.
20 Government of Canada, 'The Anti-terrorism Act', *Department of Justice*, 2001.
21 Leo Panitch, 'Violence as a Tool of Order and Change: The War on Terrorism and the Anti-Globalization Movement', *Policy Options*, September 2002, pp. 40-44; Earl, Jennifer 'Tanks, Tear Gas, and Taxes: Toward a Theory of Movement Repression', *Sociological Theory*, 2003, Vol. 21, No. 1, pp. 44-68; Aaron Doyle and Richard Ericson, 'Globalization and the Policing of Protest: The Case of APEC 1997', *The British Journal of Sociology*, 1999, Vol. 50, No. 4, pp. 589-608; James Sheptycki, 'Policing Protest When Politics Go Global: Comparing Public Order Policing in Canada and Bolivia', *Policing & Society*, 2005, Vol. 15, No. 3, pp. 327-352.
22 Following Foucault's original French usage, I take 'subjectivation' to mean the infra-constituting, active subject and how subjects become self-reflexive (which involves thinking about the stuff on which they will work) and use techniques to cultivate or make, a

self. See Michel Foucault, 'On the Genealogy of Ethics: An Overview of Work in Progress', *The Essential Foucault*, Paul Rabinow and Nikolas Rose, eds., (New York: The New Press), pp. 102-125.
23 Golder and Fitzpatrick well explicate the relationship between law and the future. For them, in a manner reminiscent of Hobbesian and Weberian constitutionalism, but without reference to Foucault's linking of law and liberalism, 'Law must necessarily attempt to plan and arrange for future events and to make some determinate provision for the future, to bring the future into the present and to actualize it in the existent. This is the idea of law incorporatively engaging with a future, bringing a future to its determinate position' (Golder and Fitzpatrick, *Foucault's Law*, pp. 131-2, n. 5). Yet, this view gives too much credence to law as a rational discourse and neglects the irrationalities of common law and political expediency in the legislative process. See also: Nikolas Rose, *Powers of Freedom* (Cambridge: Cambridge University Press, 1999); Dillon, 'Governing Through Contingency'.
24 Foucault, *Security, Territory, Population*, p. 109.
25 Michel Foucault, 'The Subject and Power', *The Essential Foucault*, eds. Paul Rabinow and Nikolas Rose (New York: The New Press, 2003), pp. 137-138.
26 Lucia Zedner, 'Pre-crime and post-criminology?', *Theoretical Criminology*, 2007, Vol. 11, No. 2, pp. 261-281; Marieke De Goede, 'Beyond Risk: Premediation and the Post-9/11 Security Imagination', *Security Dialogue*, 2008, Vol. 39, Nos. 2-3, pp. 155-176.
27 Foucault, 'Subject and Power', p. 132.
28 Foucault, *Security, Territory, Population*, p. 99.
29 Foucault, *Security, Territory, Population*, p. 105.
30 My sense is that this pervasive epistemic practice of police is now largely performed by the discourse of economics. Economics, as a discursive technology, depends on monetised market exchanges that record and transmit people's senses of values (i. e., the state of moral health of the population) in terms of prices that then become a proxy index for what classically, police aimed to do. In this regard, economics is an inherent part of apparatuses of security.
31 Marianna Valverde, 'Genealogies of European state: Foucauldian Reflections', *Economy and Society*, 2007, Vol. 36, No. 1, p.172.

32 Colin Gordon, 'Governmental Rationality: An Introduction', *The Foucault Effect: Studies in Governmentality*, in Graham Burchell *et al* (eds.), (Chicago: University of Chicago Press, 1991), p. 20.
33 Michel Foucault, *Society Must Be Defended* (New York: Picador, 2003), p. 249.
34 Thomas Osborne, 'Security and Vitality: Drains, Liberalism and Power in the Nineteenth Century', in Andrew Barry et. al., (eds), *Foucault and Political Reason*, (London: University College of London Press, 1996), p. 201.
35 Foucault, 'Subject and Power', p. 132.
36 Alan Hunt, *Explorations in Law and Society*, (New York: Routledge, 1993), p. 325.
37 Michel Foucault, *The History of Madness* (New York; Routledge, 2006); MariannaValverde, 'Despotism and Ethical Liberal Governance', *Economy and Society*, 1996, Vol. 25, No. 3, pp. 357-372.
38 Foucault, 'ON POPULAR JUSTICE'.
39 While my Foucauldian inflection on the conception of 'security fetishism', differs from that of Neocleous, I concur with his view that, 'in order to be "productive" for capital, security has to undergo the reification universally applied across the bourgeois world; security must first be translated into the materiality of the commodity'. Mark Neocleous, *Critique of Security* (Montreal and Kingston: McGill-Queen's University Press, 2008), p. 153.
40 Michel Foucault, 'Confining Societies', in *Foucault Live*, ed. Sylvere Lotringer (New York: Semiotext(e)), p. 90; cf. Foucault, 'On Popular Justice', p. 20.
41 Michel Foucault, 'The Ethics of the Concern for the Self as a Practice of Freedom', in *Essential Foucault*, p. 27.
42 See Slavoj Zizek, *The Ticklish Subject* (New York: Verso, 1999), pp. 198-205; Ernesto Laclau, *On Populist Reason* (New York: Verso, 2007), p. x.
43 Slavoj Zizek, *Iraq: the Borrowed Kettle* (New York: Verso, 2005), p. 15.
44 Mary Douglas, *Purity and Danger*, (New York: Routledge), p. 203.
45 Terry Eagleton, *Holy Terror*, (London: Oxford University Press, 2005); Michael Hardt and Antonio Negri, *Multitude*, (New York: Penguin Books, 2004), p. 16-17.

[9]
'All the People Necessary Will Die to Achieve Security'

GUILLERMINA SERI

"Tired of taking the poorest in society to prison", confessed my interviewee, an Argentine detective.[1] Many of his peers do not think the same. Being poor, they insist, is no reason to commit crimes. As if mirroring this claim, a number of poor youths report constant police harassment. Their voices, generally silenced, can be heard in human rights accounts, from testimonies gathered by researchers, in *cumbia villera* lyrics, and exceptionally also in poetry.[2] In large numbers, the victims of police violence are young, male, and poor, marked by the stigma of being *villeros*, shantytown dwellers. Some of these poor youths are threatened by the uniformed not to leave their quarters. Others narrate the experience of having members of militarised security forces patrolling their *barrio* in the way of an occupation army.[3] Hundreds of them were last seen while in police custody. Often showing signs of torture, some were found dead, killed in staged 'shootings' or 'suicides'. Like Luciano Arruga, a sixteen-year-old last seen in January 2009 when detained by the police, some remain missing. Mistreatment, violence, torture are routine.[4] Shantytowns keep memories of teenagers killed with police bullets. About four thousand arbitrary killings by the police have been documented in Argentina since the return of democracy in 1983.[5] A dark irony, almost 40 percent of these documented deaths, 1,633, took place under governments that promised not to "criminalise social protest"[6] and that made human rights a priority. And yet police violence escalated, some participants in protests saw themselves treated as criminals, and a few grassroots leaders and activists were killed in the streets by the police. Considering the population at large, in 2008, 8.70 percent Argentine survey respondents reported to have suffered verbal or physical police abuse. In 2010, in another survey, 21.05 percent declared to have witnessed street clashes between protesters and the police.[7] One would think that the people would be weary of police agents. And they are, yet they demand more police patrolling and security.

In what has turned into a mantra, many claim to be tired of getting robbed and killed. Demands for *seguridad*, conveying meanings of state security and personal safety, claiming protection from common criminals, are a top priority in public opinion surveys. Periodically, they also heighten political campaigns. Noticeably, Argentines appear to experience more insecurity than most other Latin Americans.[8] No matter that the country's homicide rate is among the lowest in the region, or that homicides may have gone down. Concerns with crime rose in the nineties, to become a priority by 2002-2003.[9] Seeing Argentines leading the cry for security seems intriguing, if one remembers our past experience with state terror, courtesy of national security agencies, after soon-to-be dictator Jorge Rafael Videla proclaimed, in 1975, "all the people necessary will die to achieve security".[10]

What insecure individuals experience as being threatened by criminals betrays broader, structural sources of fear and anxiety. Interviewed by Susana Murillo, participants in demonstrations claiming for security identified some of them. The experience of state terror, with thousands of 'disappearances' back in the seventies, 5,000 percent hyper-inflationary spikes in the late eighties, state confiscation of people's savings in 2001, unemployment, work in unstable, badly paid, legally blurry jobs, kidnappings for ransom, interpersonal violence, the loss of egalitarian values define milestones in lives "subjected to the deepest arbitrariness", Murillo notes.[11]

Prey to the whims of volatile markets and of an often unpredictable state, in fear, people demand protection. The state and the market meet their demands with security systems, guards, and police. About 250,000 police agents patrol Argentina and its population of forty million.[12] Generating profits larger than the nation's entire public security budget, at least 1,200 private security companies employ between 150,000 and 200,000.[13]

Security will not protect the people from the market, nor will it provide them with shelter, medicines, or food. Taking their hostility for granted, it just protects them from each other. An apparatus of protection, the state manufactures the hostile environment it presupposes, making the Hobbesian state of nature into a "realised fiction"[14] of devils, enemies, and threats. As a trick of statistics, in Argentina, those killed by state agents are counted as victims of 'homicide'. Their deaths paradoxically result in support for more policing. Why and how this happens is impossible to understand without addressing the bonds between state and capital.

"Life, once politicized as necessary for the continued accumulation of capital, becomes expendable at that moment when it no longer assists in the circulation of value. In this context, political inclusion remains articulated to use value for capital", Joshua Barkan rightly observes.[15] Not by revisiting political economy, however, as he contends, but through furthering its *critique*, the links between life and power come to light. As capital takes over, lives count for their potential to generate value. Or at least to consume what others generate. Those for whom the market has no room and who see themselves left out even by thin social policies, are treated as a "social residue".[16] They, the mass of the excluded, defines the main target of securitization. They are the criminals of police practices and security narratives. Security is both a device and a fetish that turns the market's victims into state enemies. Police violence against them appears as the treatment of those whose existence constitutes an *excess*, according to parameters traceable to the logic of capital.

Security, police, capital

Capital, Marx explains, is a relation between people that, as in a 'fantastic' light, to those involved appears as a relation between things. The things in question, commodities, are goods produced for exchange in the market. Capital commodifies everything it touches. It either subjects things and beings to its own rationale or excludes and destroys them. In particular, capital commodifies labour, the creative source of value. Treating every individual's labour force as a regular commodity exchangeable for money, the egalitarian terms of the labour contract hide the private appropriation of its fruits. Labour is collective; the labour contract individualises it, separating and disempowering those who work. What remains hidden, the source of value and exploitation, distorts perception. What remains hidden, the core that needs to be secured, betrays the modern roots of security. The animate exchanges places with the inanimate in the "personification of things and reification of the relations of production".[17] It happens as in a '*camera obscura*', Marx observes.[18] The social world turns upside down. Starting with the commodity, fetishes arise. People appear as passively subjected to things that seem to have a life of their own. Commodity fetishism, "the capitalist symptom",[19] anchors other fetishes or reified social relations. Exuding their little halos and speaking little voices, they govern our lives.

The state is one of them. An "aspect",[20] "surface", "form",[21] and 'node' of capital, in the business of reproducing capital's web of relations, the state confronts us as an agent with personality.[22] Constantly forming and reproducing, capital, commodities, money, and the state acquire their definite "thing-like shell".[23] The state, as Giorgio Agamben noted, has its foundation not in a social bond but in its dissolution.[24] Separating individuals defines "the source of the Leviathan's power"[25]; Separating individuals lays the foundation of capital. Internalizing Hobbesian traits, individuals turn isolated, hostile, and insecure. Leviathan's *homo naturalis* is the *homo economicus* of capital.

Mercantile subjectivities need to be made and remade. Commodified desire, compulsive consumption, and the conceptual couplet fear-and-security stand as main self-governing modalities.[26] As individuals live in fear, and the fearful demand more protection, security acts as a fishhook in which they get further entrapped. In theory, capital relies solely on such automatic mechanisms. Not much is automatic, however, when labour organises, or monopolies need to be preserved. The market only reproduces what the state alone guarantees. It all starts with property, the private property of the means of production, code for capital's security.

Half public good, half 'special commodity' secreting fear, security, as Mark Neocleous and George Rigakos note in *Anti-Security: A Declaration*, "operates as the supreme concept of bourgeois society". Security protects the social relation of capital. To capital owners, security's public provision permits to prorate the cost of better trained, professionalised forces.[27] In this light, as a collectively subsidised service, the uniformed police agent complements the work of private guards.

If the state is a dimension of capital, police is the social relation that condenses the state. Each police agent amounts to a link in a dense web of police organizations and exercises of police power, with visible and invisible arrangements in the surveillance of individuals and groups. They are, an Argentine commissioner explains, the ones who "guarantee security in the streets". At a micro-scale, on a one-to-one basis, the police help in the production and reproduction of state and social bonds. Their force accelerates "the accumulation of capital by increasing the degree of exploitation of labour",[28] as Marx put it. But there is more than that. Far from merely repressive, the police offer of unconditional protection gathers them consent. "To serve the people, without making any distinction...from the richest to the poorest ones...without distinctions of any kind... To serve the public totally". Expressing similar commitments than my Argentine Federal Police interviewee, whether candidly or out of strategic reasons police agents appropriate demands for care and translate them into matters of security and police.

Spreading out in society, reaching inside homes and souls, offering care, brandishing the law, and carrying a gun, with discretion to judge which one to use, every police agent embodies a minute replica of the state. Like alchemists, they recode care as security. Through them, the state takes over the governance of conflicts. If the state shows us one face of capital, the police are the state's most condensed governing organ, an appropriate mirror to reach the state's heart.

'Let me see your ID'

"At the basis of an immensely complex social structure lies a simple principle – identity", John Holloway contends.[29] Mercantile production and exchange require simple, stable selves to affix ownership and financial and criminal responsibility. Public and private systems of surveillance and security fix us onto them. The state, in particular, as Agamben noted, needs to place individuals "in some identity, whatever identity".[30] Those who do not fit its discrete categories are turned into its "principal enemy".[31] Underneath identity's apparent 'explosion' of vocal women, ethnic or cultural minorities, or gays and lesbians, we find a common language of IDs, nationality, passports, addresses, and credit and criminal records.[32] They act as passwords for the inclusion of the selected few. They let the life suited to capital circulate.

Present-day democracies nominally acknowledge most citizens as free political agents. The effective exercise of rights, however, which Hannah Arendt referred to as the right to have rights,[33] seems contingent to *de iure* and *de facto* recognition by the state. If channeled through different state apparatuses, to a considerable extent the access to rights relies on everyday police decisions. Administering force and gathering consent, the police help to reproduce individuals as disciplined producers and consumers. In so doing, agents have leeway to move outside the law, invade our privacy, and fake identities themselves. "We are part of everything, if only we are not specific", refers an officer from the Federal Police. Formless and alegal, police power freezes us onto definite identities and webs of the law.

Through policies in part formal, in part informal, moving on dubiously legal, alegal, or illegal grounds, the police differentiate people along hierarchies of worth. Acting as gatekeepers of rights, citizenship, and humanity, police agents sort individuals into categories accessing rights and others to be securitised, criminalised, and governed only on the basis of force. In the end, those stigmatised as 'undesirable' find themselves turned into a threat. Through the police routine of "distinguishing criminals from citizens", P.A.J. Waddington explains, "the exercise of coercive authority can be conducted almost without restraint".[34] As everyday policing exposes, the direct governance of life through hierarchies of belonging, dignity, and rights traditionally associated with sovereigns constitutes a widespread, routine police task.[35] Among us, the rationale of capital helps to make intelligible the state dynamics of identification, its violence, and the governmental practices articulating them.

The state, as Neocleous and Rigakos note, dismantles "all that is inherently communal", to reshape interpersonal bonds in terms of "state rationality, corporate interest, and individual egoism". Lives and selves, as Holloway describes, are left "shattered into so many identities, so many cold atoms of existence, standing each one on its own".[36] Following their disarticulation, selves and groups find themselves reified into artificial collectives and standardised figures. Rhetorical unification provides cohesion, at least ideological one. In the end, individuals learn to imagine themselves as the people of a nation, deemed the ultimate, most genuine kinship containing all others.

By making distinctions between categories of the (in)human, the police contribute to define the nation and to patrol its internal borders and zones of lawlessness. As individuals internalise them, the nation, identity, and security come into existence also as part of our selves.[37] Like the humans turned into living batteries in the film *The Matrix*, millions of lives feed forces that seem beyond our control and that determine our fate. And yet, immersed within its web, prey to contingent capital moves, we tend to experience this systemic danger normalised as insecurity crises, scapegoating some of the state and capital's own victims.

Civilizing and pacifying

"To civilize is to project police power", note Neocleous and Rigakos; police power diffuses capital. For the last five centuries, the planet has seen their combined expansion.[38] Through brutal transformations, like that of peasants into starving poor and industrial workers in England recalled by Marx, capital took over even the most distant corners on earth.[39] In so doing, it structured a system of states and multiple layers of wealthy centres and poorer peripheries. In contrast to the first European societies where it took centuries for capital to develop, the speed of its expansion made the process more openly violent and exclusionary in the periphery, as Gilberto Mathias and Pierre Salama noted.

This seems clear in modern Argentina, organised in a couple of decades to provide agricultural goods to the metropolis undergoing its second industrial revolution. In a few years, Buenos Aires turned into a satellite of London, its manufactures succumbed to British commodities, the richest land in the Pampas was forcefully taken, and previously prosperous regional hubs ruined as they were subjected to the world market following these shifts.

The genocide of the indigenous people through 'civilising' military campaigns 'to the Desert', intermittent civil war with recalcitrant regional forces, and the largest South American war crowned the endeavour.[40] With the help of London, André Gunder Frank recalls, Buenos Aires, Montevideo, and Rio de Janeiro "destroyed not only the autonomously developing economy of Paraguay but killed off nearly all its population which was unwilling to give in".⁴¹ When the task was completed, the founders of modern Argentina brought a mass of the exceeding European proletariat to put them to work. Under exceptional conditions of production and exploitation, Argentina became one of the wealthiest countries in the world.⁴²

It takes both mercantile and non-mercantile means to fiercely discipline resilient populations, and to *secure* lives, space, and labour to the movements of capital. Built around an export-oriented scheme, the extension of Argentina's labour market has been in question since then, as has the inclusiveness of its polity. More than once the powerful showed no hesitation in banning people from citizenship, more than once also proceeding to their physical annihilation. It is the security of capital.

At different levels, the state's police power recreates the classifying, labelling, and destruction of life. At times, it may take the annihilation of the indigenous peoples, or the eventual destruction of the entire male population of Paraguay. At times, it takes mass deportations of activists, the execution of industrial and rural workers,⁴³ ruthless military dictatorship, or making a generation 'disappear'. At times, in 'normal' times, it may be just the chasing of a poor teenager. The docility of the poor that economic and social policies can achieve in a fully waged society invites additional state violence in incompletely commodified territories. All the more the more seriously the people take modernity's promise of freedom and rights.

Even before the 1929 crisis, in Argentina, import substitution industrialization began to give visibility to an organised working class. Starting in the thirties, the powerful banned political rights for the masses, whether indirectly or overthrowing elected governments through *coups d'état*. Even representative democracy seemed insecure to the elites for preserving the security of capital. In 1966, to counter popular resistance, a military dictatorship passed a national security law letting the state define individuals as internal enemies. Whose security could be possibly threatened by individual citizens under a military dictatorship?

'The people', formal and informal workers alike, resisted and mobilised. Confronting repression, they fought for rights, elections, while they organised and coordinated factory councils.[44] By mid 1975, a large number of workers went on a general strike.[45] Ensuing calls to repress what was called 'factory guerrilla' signed the fate of thousands of workers in anticipation to the most ferocious 1976 *coup d'état*. It then became clear what General Videla had meant when promising that all the people necessary would die to achieve security.

Institutionalised after the coup, state terror manifested earlier, with police-sponsored death squadrons such as those of the Anticommunist Argentine Alliance, responsible for 1,500 political murders between 1973 and 1975.[46] After March, 1976, squadrons took tens of thousands of individuals from the streets, their homes or workplace to hundreds of clandestine death camps, making them 'disappear'. Labelled subversives, whose ideas, politics, and lifestyle were said to threaten the Christian and Western, they were treated as non-Argentine, 'no persons', as a pest. Thus, in Argentina, the "turn towards neoliberalism"[47] in the seventies, an attempt to regain control by the owners of capital, came together with death squads.

It would be only years later, in a restored democracy struggling with debt crises and negative growth, that as if echoing lessons learned through the pedagogy of terror many judged the market the solution. One of the fullest experiences of deregulation and privatization ensued. In a longer span, considering the period 1976-1992, Argentina offered the extraordinary rate of 72 percent in equity returns, reaching 88 percent between 1985 and 1992, the highest in the financial international market.[48] Financial capital, we know, does not create value, but only redistribute what others create. As powerful voices raised concerns about 'juridical security', the security of capital was given guarantees.

After a generation had been decimated, a couple of others underwent the ferocious disciplining of labour deregulation, poverty, and unemployment. Hundreds of thousands lost their jobs, healthcare, and retirement pensions, unemployment reached 'unprecedented' levels, and even the few luckier accessed a flimsy labour market. Fear of crime escalated.[49] Demands for protection led to larger federal and provincial security budgets, the legal and illegal increase of firearms, and the rapid expansion of private security firms.

In December 2001, both the market and the country collapsed. Billions of dollars fled, accompanied by their owners, while banks, corporations, and the state sacked the common people. Precipitated by wild, unregulated markets, the living conditions of millions dissolved. Poverty, which in 1974 stood around 4 percent, had climbed to at least 54.3 by 2002.[50] Only the captains of capital remained *secure*. "There is justice for the poor and justice for the wealthy", observed a young police officer. 'Touching' white collar crime is 'very difficult'. While many people got to question neoliberalism, others became obsessed with common crime.

Rising from the ashes of the country's bankruptcy, with booming agricultural exports and reindustrialization, economic recovery was fast and dramatic. Yet, not even at its peak, after seven years of around 8 percent annual GDP growth, the market seemed able to absorb those who had been left out, between a third and a half of the population of forty million. With more than one third of all workers in the informal market, and many informal workers living at the brinks of destitution,[51] social programs reach out to keep them afloat. In the meantime, media scandals expose the scope of servitude and *de facto* slavery in the pampas.[52]

As society turns structurally unequal and commonalities wane, *seguridad* offers the articulation of its fragments as a community united under the threat of crime. A hidden enemy, the criminal, lurks over the decent. Transforming social victims into dangerous suspects, the nation reimagines itself. Insecurity perceptions, fear of crime? No surprise, they continue growing. As has piecemeal police violence targeting the young and poor.

The state as police

Communities, Esposito notes, develop from the reciprocal recognition of what people lack and need, out of a mutual search for care.[53] State agents and the police appropriate and transform this demand for care into security. In a seminal study bridging the sociological, the historical, and the archaeological, Cyril Robinson and Richard Scaglion identify the origins of the police function in the passage from stateless to state societies. Claiming to reproduce kinship while appealing to its horizontal, egalitarian values, early-specialized police agents, the authors explain, carried out a transformation by replacing communal social control with state-led hierarchical, bureaucratised patron-client ties.[54] As a result, individuals saw themselves involved in a vertical relation of obedience in exchange for protection, or clientage, which became the basis of the state.[55] Similarly, Michel Foucault identifies ways in which since the 12th century the sovereign, and eventually also the bureaucracy around him, 'confiscated' the administration of conflict, by forcing themselves as offended party in all disputes between individuals.[56]

In the perennial dance between ontogenesis and phylogenesis, police agents continue helping to expropriate the administration of both care and conflict that gave origin to the state. Creating opportunities for state governance, through minute interventions across society, the police co-opt, neutralise, illegalise, or destroy alternative arrangements. As communal forms of production, ownership, social control, and care of life are disarticulated or criminalised by the state, and yet the market does not absorb more workers, many see themselves turned "into vagabonds and paupers",[57] thrown outside the law, rights, and humanity, spatially abandoned in poor enclaves, or killed.

Security now clothes itself with citizenship, as 'citizen' security. Different policies, granted, may be more or less conducive to violence. But, as the confluence of a government committed to human rights with mounting killings by the police has shown these years in Argentina, both capital and state apparatuses place structural limits even to good souls. Moreover, police support for democracy has its limits. The police remain vigilant against revolution. Of course, an Argentine detective declares, the police would not support a future attempt of *coup*, as the past "left just regrets and deaths". This is, unless "God forbids, the country has a revolution. For whatever reason, that would be a different thing". This may be the reason why, in the perspective of the police 'social defence', the line between criminal and political intelligence remains blurry, even when political intelligence is illegal for most police forces to do.[58] Capital, as Holloway rightly points out, "exists not because we created it in the 19th century or in the 18th century or whenever. Capitalism exists today only because we created it today".[59] The Cold War may be over, but capital needs to be recreated every day, and there are always unruly subjects in the global kingdom of state and capital.

Notes
1   Interviews with police officers held between 2001 and 2008 in Argentina by the author.
2   Osvaldo Quintana, 'Lobo suelto, cordero atado', *El Colectivo*, 15 May, 2007; 'Es más peligroso un pibe que piensa que un pibe que roba', *Pagina12*, November 2010; Cristian Alarcón, *Cuando me muera quiero que me toquen cumbia. Vidas de pibes chorros* (Buenos Aires: Norma, 19th reimpression, 2007). Camilo Blajaquis, who has moved from life as a *villero* youth to gaining recognition as a poet, is one of the rare voices who speaks for these youths.
3   Sebastián Vricella, 'La muerte me tiene re-zarpado', *Crisis*, February/March 2011, pp. 23-27.
4   United Nations Committee against Torture, 'Issues Concluding Observations on Reports of Argentina, the United Kingdom and Greece' - www.unhchr.ch/huricane/huricane.nsf/view01/11C1DB0E9EBC2772C125 6F58005032E7?opendocument; Amnesty International, *Argentina: Implementation of the United Nations Convention against Torture and other Cruel, Inhuman or Degrading Treatment or Punishment*, 31 January, 2005.
5   CORREPI, *Presentación del Archivo 2010* (Buenos Aires: November 20, 2010).
6   'No quiero criminalizar la protesta social', *Clarín*, 3 June, 2003.
7   *The Latin American Public Opinion Project* (LAPOP), Vanderbilt University - lapop.ccp.ucr.ac.cr; Argentina, 2008, question Vic27; LAPOP, Argentina 2010, question argprot7.
8   *Informe Latino barómetro 2010*, p. 8 - www.latinobarometro.org. Both in 2008 and 2010 respondents judged crime to be the most important problem in the region.
9   Interview with Gabriel Kessler, *La Pulseada* 85 (La Plata: Argentina, December 2010).
10 'Si es preciso en la Argentina deberán morir todas las personas necesarias para lograr la seguridad del país' - Jorge Rafael Videla, speaking at the Eleventh Inter-American Army Conference, Montevideo, La Nación, October 26, 1975, cited in Oscar Anzorena, *Tiempo de violencia y utopía: de Golpe de Onganía (1966) and Golpe de Videla (1976)* (Buenos Aires: Ediciones del Pensamiento Nacional, 1998), p. 324.
11 Susana Murillo, *Colonizar el dolor: La interpelación ideológica del Banco Mundial en América Latina. El caso argentino desde Blumberg a Cromañón* (Buenos Aires: CLACSO, 2008), p. 175.

12　OAS, *La Seguridad Pública en las Américas: retos y oportunidades* (OAS Official Records Series, 2008).
13　Edgardo Frigo, *Seguridad Privada en Latinoamérica: Situación y Perspectivas*. Mimeo, 2006, qtd.by Lucía Dammert, *Seguridad Privada: ¿Respuesta a las necesidades de seguridad pública en conglomerados urbanos?* OAS, 2008, p. 5; 'El negocio de la inseguridad', *Crítica,* 13 December, 2009.
14　Marcelo Matellanes, *Del Maltrato Social* (Buenos Aires; Ediciones Cooperativas, 2003), p. 59.
15　Joshua Barkan, 'Use Beyond Value: Giorgio Agamben and a Critique of Capitalism', *Rethinking Marxism,* Volume 21, Issue 2, 2009, pp. 243 – 259.
16　Alcira Daroqui, (ed.) *Muertes silenciadas: La eliminación de los 'delincuentes'* (Buenos Aires: Ediciones del CCC, 2009).
17　Karl Marx, *Capital: A Critique of Political Economy, Vol. 3,* trans. David Fernbach (London: Penguin, 1981), p. 969.
18　Karl Marx, 'From *The German Ideology,* Volume One', *The Portable Karl Marx,* ed. Eugene Kamenka (London: Penguin, 1983), p. 169.
19　Paul-Laurent Assoun, *El Fetichismo,* (Buenos Aires: Nueva Vision, 1995), p. 48.
20　John Holloway and Sol Picciotto 'Capital, Crisis and the State', *Capital & Class* , Vol. 1, 1977, pp. 76-101, p. 76.
21　Holloway and Picciotto, 'Capital, Crisis and the State', p. 77.
22　Gilberto Mathias and Pierre Salama, *El Estado Sobredesarrollado* (Mexico; Era, 1983), p. 24.
23　Rosdolsky, cited in Holloway and Picciotto, 'Capital, Crisis and the State', p. 76.
24　Giorgio Agamben, *The Coming Community* (Minneapolis: University of Minnesota Press, 1993), p. 86.
25　James Der Derian, 'The Value of Security', *On Security* (R. Lipschutz ed.; New York: Columbia University Press, 1995).
26　Herbert Marcuse, *One-Dimensional Man: Studies in the Ideology of Advanced Industrial Society* (Boston: Beacon Press, 1991); Guy Debord, *The Society of the Spectacle* (Zone Books, D. Nicholson-Smith trans., 1994); Michel Foucault, *The Birth of Biopolitics* (New York: Palgrave, 2007).
27　Immanuel Wallerstein, *The Modern World System: Capitalist Agriculture and the Origins of the European World-Economy in the Sixteenth Century* (New York: Academic Press, 1976).

28 Karl Marx, *Capital: A Critique of Political Economy, Vol. I*, trans. Ben Fowkes (London: Penguin, 1992), p. 905.
29 John Holloway, *Change the World Without Taking Power* (London: Pluto Press, 2005), p. 68.
30 Agamben, *The Coming Community*, p. 86.
31 Agamben, *The Coming Community*, p. 87.
32 James Scott, *Seeing Like a State* (New Haven: Yale University Press, 2000), pp. 66, 220, 371; Benedict Anderson, *Imagined Communities* (London: Verso, 1983), p. 204; Mark Neocleous, *Imagining the State* (Berkshire and Philadelphia: McGraw-Hill International, 2003), p. 52.
33 Hannah Arendt, 'The Perplexities of the Rights of Man', in *The Portable Hannah Arendt*, ed. Peter R. Baehr (New York: Penguin Classics, 2003).
34 P.A.J. Waddington, 'Police (Canteen) Sub-culture: An Appreciation'. *British Journal of Criminology* 89(2), 1999, p. 300.
35 Giorgio Agamben, 'Sovereign Police, in *Means without Ends* (Minneapolis: University of Minnesota Press, 2000), p. 103; *Homo Sacer* (Stanford: Stanford University Press, 1998), p. 6.
36 Holloway, *Change the World*, p. 73.
37 Mark Neocleous, *Critique of Security* (Edinburgh: Edinburgh University Press, 2008), p. 107; Balibar, Etienne. 'The Nation Form', in Etienne Balibar and Immanuel Wallerstein, *Race, Nation, Class: Ambiguous Identities* (London: Verso, 1991), pp. 102, 93, 94.
38 Wallerstein, *Modern World-System*.
39 André Gunder Frank, *Imperialism and Underdevelopment* (New York: Monthly Press, 1970), p. 4.
40 Tulio Halperin Donghi, *The Contemporary History of Latin America* (Durham: Duke University Press, 1993), p. 134.
41 Gunder Frank, *Imperialism*.
42 Halperin Donghi, *Contemporary History*, pp. 122, 172.
43 Halperin Donghi, *Contemporary History*, p. 190.
44 Adolfo Gilly, 'La anomalía argentina (estado, corporaciones y trabajadores)', *El Estado en America Latina: teoría y practica* (Pablo González Casanova ed, Mexico: Siglo XXI, 1990).
45 Eduardo Sartelli, 'Argentina, general strike, 1975', in Immanuel Ness (ed.), *The International Encyclopedia of Revolution and Protest* (Malden: Wiley-Blackwell, 2009).

46 Wolfgang Heinz, 'Determinants of Gross Human Rights Violations by State and State-sponsored Actors in Argentina 1976-1983', in Wolfgang S. Heinz and Hugo Frühling (eds), *Determinants of Gross Human Rights Violations by State and State-sponsored Actors in Brazil, Uruguay, Chile, and Argentina, 1960-1990* (Martinus Nijhoff Publishers, 1999).

47 Ronaldo Munck, 'Neoliberalism, Necessitarianism and Alternatives in Latin America: There is No Alternative (TINA)', *Third World Quarterly*, Vol. 24, No. 3, 2003, 495-511, p. 496.

48 Campbell R. Harvey, 'The Risk of Exposure of Emerging Equity Markets', *The World Bank Economic Review*, Vol. 9, No 1, 1995, p. 22-23.

49 Gabriela Benza and Gabriel Calvi, 'Desempleo y precariedad laboral en el origen de la desigualdad de ingresos personales. Estudiando el legado distributivo de los años '90', *Lavboratorio/n line*, Year 6, No 17-18, 2005.

50 Mario Brodersohn, 'Dos Grandes Mitos del Peronismo: Sabe Gobernar y ser el Partido de la Justicia Social', *Econométrica*, September 2009, p. 6 - www.offnews.info/downloads/EconometricaMensualSeptiembre2009.pdf

51 Eduardo M. Basualdo, 'La reestructuración de la economía argentina durante las últimas décadas de la sustitución de importaciones a la valorización financiera', *Neoliberalismo y sectores dominantes. Tendencias globales y experiencias nacionales* , in Eduardo M. Basualdo and Enrique Arceo (eds), (Buenos Aires: CLACSO, 2006), pp. 166, 170-1; Gustavo Ludmer, 'Salarios y distribución', *Pagina12*, 7 February, 2011; Mario Santucho, 'Una nueva composición social', *Crisis* 3, 2011.

52 Horacio Verbitsky, 'Trabajo esclavo para una trader cerealera evasora', *Pagina12,* January 2, 2011; Exequiel Siddig, 'No compre trabajo esclavo', *Miradas al Sur* 142. 6 February, 2011.

53 Roberto Esposito, *Communitas: The Origin and Destiny of Community* (Stanford: Stanford University Press, 2009), p. 96.

54 Cyril D. Robinson and Richard Scaglion. 'The Origin and Evolution of the Police Function in Society: Notes Toward a Theory', *Law and Society Review* Vol. 21 No 1, 1987, pp. 112-3, 118, 131.

55 Esposito, *Communitas*, p. 28.

56 Michel Foucault, 'Truth and Juridical Forms', *Power: Essential Works of Foucault 1954-1984*, ed. James D. Faubion (New York: The New Press, 2000).

57 Marx, *Capital*, p. 896.
58 Paul Chevigny, *The Edge of The Knife: Police Violence in the Americas* (New York: The New Press, 1995); Laura Kalmanowiecki, 'Origins and Applications of Political Policing in Argentina'. *Latin American Perspectives* Vol. 27, March 2000, pp. 36-56.
59 John Holloway, 'Change the World Without Taking Power', Transcription of a video by O. Ressler, *EIPCP*, Vienna, Austria, 2004 - eipcp.net/transversal/0805/holloway/en.

Notes on Contributors

Ronjon Paul Datta is Assistant Professor of Social Theory and Cultural Studies in the Department of Sociology at The University of Alberta. He specialises in contemporary and classical social theory, the philosophy of social science, political formations and the sociology of the sacred. Recent publications discuss Agamben, Bataille, Foucault, Durkheim, Critical Realism, social justice and the political economy of debt. Current research concerns cosmopolitanism, justice, Foucault and sociological metatheory, power and neo-Foucauldian conceptions of politics.

Gaétan Héroux is an anti-poverty activist and a member of the Ontario Coalition Against Poverty who has worked and organized around issues of poverty in East Downtown Toronto for more than twenty years.

Will Jackson is a doctoral candidate at the University of Salford, UK. His thesis is concerned with the politics of liberty and security and seeks to provide a critical analysis of the function human rights fulfil in the context of the 'war on terror'. Rather than understanding the relationship between human rights and security as developed and sustained solely at the level of state or government action in this period, his work has a central concern with the crucial role played by certain intellectual strata and human rights advocacy organisations in constructing and legitimating the current liberty-security regime.

Michael Kempa holds a Doctorate in Law awarded through the Australian National University. Working within the Department of Criminology, University of Ottawa, his research addresses the ways in which states and non-state organizations variously conceive of and attempt to institutionalize 'police power'. He is passionate about the potential for studying and teaching social theory to develop opportunities for students and citizens to engage planetary renewal through the opportunity structures available to them.

Olena Kobzar teaches 'Law and Society' at York University, Toronto, and is completing her PhD at the Centre of Criminology and Socio Legal Studies at the University of Toronto. Her PhD shows that the regulatory environment for the payday loan industry is informed by contradictory assumptions drawn from an older conception of a moral economy and modern conceptions of the market economy, creating an air of incoherence, if not futility, to policy initiatives in this area.

Mark Neocleous is Professor of the Critique of Political Economy at Brunel University, UK, and on the Editorial Collective of the journal *Radical Philosophy*. He is author of *Critique of Security* (2008), *The Fabrication of Social Order: A Critical Theory of Police Power* (2000), and a range of other books and articles. He is currently working on a project of counter-strategic theory.

George S. Rigakos is Chair of Law and Legal Studies at Carleton University and Editor of Red Quill Books. He has published on public and private policing; policing and social theory; and theorizing risk. Rigakos' books include *Nightclub: Bouncers, Risk and the Spectacle of Consumption* (2008), *A General Police System* (2009), *The New Parapolice* (2002) and an edited four-part illustrated series on *The Communist Manifesto* (2010-11).

Heidi Rimke is an Associate Professor in the Department of Sociology at the University of Winnipeg, Canada. She specializes in the areas of classical and contemporary social and political thought, critical criminology, and the history of the human sciences with a focus on 'psy' discourses/practices.

Guillermina Seri is an Assistant Professor of Latin American politics and political theory at Union College, Schenectady, NY. Seri's research explores the governing aspects embedded in policing, with a focus on the impact of grassroots police practices on the form of regime. Her book *Seguridad, Crime, Police Power, and Democracy in Argentina*, is forthcoming with Continuum Press.

CPSIA information can be obtained at www.ICGtesting.com
Printed in the USA
BVOW032307191212

308669BV00001B/3/P